FT.com
FINANCIAL TIMES

books for the future minded

Welcome to the next generation of business

There is a new world which we can look at but we cannot see. Yet within it, the forces of technology and imagination are overturning the way we work and the way we do business.

ft.com books are both gateway and guide to this world. We understand it because we are part of it. But we also understand the needs of businesses which are taking their first steps into it, and those still standing hesitantly on the threshold. Above all, we understand that, as with all business challenges, the key to success lies not with the technology itself, but with the people who must use it and manage it. People like you – the future minded.

See a world of business.

Visit **www.ft.com** today.

managing.com

entrepreneurial business and wired
management. start here

Fredrik Arnander

FT.com
FINANCIAL TIMES

books for the
future minded An imprint of **Pearson Education**

London ■ New York ■ San Francisco ■ Toronto ■ Sydney ■ Tokyo ■ Singapore
Hong Kong ■ Cape Town ■ Madrid ■ Amsterdam ■ Munich ■ Paris ■ Milan

PEARSON EDUCATION LIMITED

Head Office:
Edinburgh Gate
Harlow CM20 2JE
Tel: +44 (0)1279 623623
Fax: +44 (0)1279 431059

London Office:
128 Long Acre, London WC2E 9AN
Tel: +44 (0)207 447 2000
Fax: +44 (0)207 240 5771
Website: www.business-minds.com

First published in Great Britain in 2001

© Pearson Education Limited 2001
The right of Fredrik Arnander to be identified as Author
of this Work has been asserted by him in accordance
with the Copyright, Designs and Patents Act 1988.

ISBN 1903 68301 7

British Library Cataloguing in Publication Data
A CIP catalogue record for this book can be obtained from the British Library

10 9 8 7 6 5 4 3 2 1

Designed by Claire Brodmann Book Designs, Lichfield, Staffs
Typeset by Pantek Arts Ltd, Maidstone, Kent
Printed and bound in Great Britain by Biddles Ltd, Guildford & King's Lynn

The Publishers' policy is to use paper manufactured from sustainable forests.

By car, by plane, they come. They just show up. They've given up their lives elsewhere to come here. They come for the tremendous opportunity, believing that in no other place in the world right now can one person accomplish so much with talent, initiative, and a good idea.

PO BRONSON,

The Nudist on the Late Shift – And Other True Tales of Silicon Valley

about the author

Fredrik Arnander was formerly a management consultant, and has also been a partner at the global web agency Icon Medialab, which started in Sweden in 1996. In 1998, he founded Fondex, one of Europe's first supermarkets for mutual funds on the internet. He sold the company in 2000 to become a member of the international executive team at Moneyextra.com, the UK's leading portal for personal finance. Today, Fredrik Arnander sits on several boards in start-ups and is engaged in new ventures. He is also the founder of Transfer, a non-profit organization for knowledge sharing between schools and the high-tech industry.

Managing.com is his second book, and his first to be published in English.

'*Managing.com* is about managing and leading in a chaotic and dynamic environment. It's based on the hard lessons of starting and growing internet companies. So this is a handbook about the things we learned, about what works and what doesn't. About managing the future, day by day.'

Fredrik Arnander

contents

welcome to the movement!

This book is based on insider knowledge from entrepreneural business in a super-turbulent market. It is a handbook for management in a new economy with a practical approach. Or, call it a framework. It's for managers with a will to change, regardless of whether it is an old company, a start-up or an entire market. It's based on ten areas that you have to master. **It starts with you**.

Leadership

How are you as a person, as a leader? How do you respond to fast-changing markets? Before you embark on new ventures in a chaotic environment, know yourself first.

Action

OK, so you have a brilliant idea and you're ready to rock. All you need now is to start, which is probably the hardest part. Regardless of whether you're a senior manager in an established company or a entrepreneur with a start-up, the challenges are the same. You've got to take the first step. You've got to start. The definitive consequence of the new economy is that only two kinds of companies can really succeed. The start-ups and the re-starts.

People

You're not alone. An ideas economy needs many different competencies to make ideas come true, and you have to realize that most of that knowledge is in someone else's head. Work with the best.

Workplace

Even though the networked economy offers new views on the concepts of time and space, there will always be a physical location where you and your team of smart people create growth. This location is your workplace and you are going to spend a lot of time there. Make it your favorite place to be.

Culture A company without a culture is like a nightclub without a beat. Your company's culture is what guides you in the chaotic landscape that is your market.

Interaction Human interaction is becoming increasingly complex with a myriad of new media through which we communicate. You have to be a master of all the surfaces that surround your company.

Business The way we do business is both changing and returning to its roots. Today, even the most seasoned board of directors can be heard discussing 'wireless' and 'websites'. How do you do the new thing?

Customers They are the ones who decide how fast your business will grow. And they have more power than ever. Welcome to the new community.

Communication In an ideas economy, you're the storyteller. If you want to take others with you into your future, you have to have a vision of where you are going. The economy is actually a battleground for ideas, and the best sales person usually wins.

Failures Be prepared to fail, and learn how to fail. At the same time, learn how to avoid mistakes.

This is a handbook. But it's also my story, and it might not work for others. In a dynamic economy, ultimately you have to write your own handbook. But I hope this book will serve as a learning experience, inspiration and, of course, entertainment.

Fredrik Arnander
Stockholm, May 2001

CHAPTER ONE

Leadership: the CEO as DJ

THERE ARE ALWAYS TWO PARTIES,

THE PARTY OF THE PAST AND

THE PARTY OF THE FUTURE,

THE ESTABLISHMENT

AND THE MOVEMENT.

RALPH WALDO EMERSON,
PHILOSOPHER

The ruthless ideas economy

Before 1970, few companies ever reached a market value over $100 million, and it was a sensation when in the 1980s computer company Compaq was valued after five years at $1 billion. Netscape started in 1994 and reached a market value of $1 billion. In just one year.

At its peak, Netscape Navigator dominated almost the whole market for web browsers, the software that made the web a commercial medium. Then on December 7 1995 software giant Microsoft finally decided that they too were an internet company. I remember that day because I happened to be at a newly started company in Stockholm called Spray. (The company grew to become a leading internet conglomerate with operations all over Europe and in the USA and with businesses including consulting, media and e-commerce. They merged with portal company Lycos in autumn 2000.) Someone ran into the room and told the news, which was about the software giant's historical change of strategy.

Suddenly it became clear that the internet was developing so fast that even the world's largest information technology company almost missed it. While Microsoft was concentrating on its Disk Operating System for PCs, some-one else was busy connecting those computers. And because that idea was better than Microsoft's, Microsoft decided to quickly develop their own browser, the Internet Explorer.

Thereafter it didn't matter how fast Netscape ran, Microsoft was getting ahead by integrating their browser into the millions of Microsoft Office software packages sold every year. *That* idea was actually better than giving the program away for free and letting users download it over the internet. Microsoft became so dominant that US courts threatened to split the company, as they did with AT&T when they became too powerful. The struggle over the mighty Microsoft continues.

But then, back in 1998, Microsoft won, Netscape lost and in 1999 the company was sold to America Online (AOL), which meanwhile had emerged as one of the world's largest media corporations, with over 20 million interactive members, and ranked as one of the 20 most valuable companies in the world. And when AOL bought Netscape it wasn't actually to get the rights to its browser, but to gain access to the vast amount of traffic on Netscape's homepage Netcenter. In 1999 the dominating idea was neither to give away web browsers for free nor to integrate them into Office software, but to aggregate as many web users as possible in the same place, a portal. What browser people used to get there became irrelevant.

Then, in 2000, we said that it didn't matter how much traffic or how many people you could gather at a portal or at any other website, as long as they were buying and generating revenue streams that could turn into positive cash flow. In 2000, the internet was about profits, like any other business.

Netscape never reached what is generally called the maturity stage of a business. They were in a hyper-speed start-up phase for four years, lost it all during the fifth and more or less disappeared (a curve that later became common among dot coms with hyper growth and rapid death). During this time spectacular market value was created, the world witnessed a new phenomenon and a new industry was born. The Netscape brand lives on as a web page and as a legend for many people that started to surf the world wide web with the first primitive version of the Netscape Navigator.

The establishment and the movement

Regardless of whether you are an internet company or any other company, the reality today is that your market space is an unpredictable environment where new ideas compete. You can't be a traditional company doing business in an untraditional environment. You can't be part of the movement and think like the establishment.

Think about rafting, you have to paddle faster than the running water to be able to steer, otherwise the chaos of the water will take command of you. To manage on the edge of chaos is to control chaos. To control chaos you have to understand chaos, and always be one step ahead.

When we talk about competition in the ideas economy, it is not competition in the ordinary sense. A typical form of competition is when car companies launch their new models and all the companies hope/believe/wish that their own models will be the choice of the consumers; but regardless of who wins, the models will co-exist side by side. The ideas economy is far more ruthless. There is a tendency to completely smash the old idea with a new idea, where the old vanishes and the new is king, the way B2B (business to business) smashed B2C (business to consumer) and the re-born idea of profitability smashed dot coms, and in the process killed many companies or reduced their market value by up to 80–90 percent. Welcome to the new world.

> "THERE IS A TENDENCY TO COMPLETELY SMASH THE OLD IDEA WITH A NEW IDEA, WHERE THE OLD VANISHES AND THE NEW IS KING"

Linus Torvalds created the operating system Linux – free to download, like Navigator – which challenged Microsoft's Disk Operating System, the global standard, The Establishment. Large resources are not needed to compete in the ideas economy in order to accomplish large changes. We don't know yet if Linux, The Movement in this example, will beat MS-DOS, but sometimes it's enough just to become a symbol of the new idea to make things happen. The Movement is usually symbolic before it becomes reality, and eventually, the Establishment.

❝Who are the Explorers and the Netscapes of your industry? Who represents the Establishment and where does the Movement come from? As a business leader, the first thing to decide is whether you're part of history or part of the future. Or both.❞

Small and big companies

In the autumn of 1999, one of the world's largest companies bought into one of the smallest. It wasn't news that created big headlines in the *Financial Times*, but it was a big thing for me. GE Equity, the venture capital branch of GE Capital and part of the American conglomerate General Electric, acquired 20 percent of Fondex, the internet-based fund supermarket I co-founded in April 1998.

For Fondex it was a question of allying the company with a global strategic partner for our international expansion. For GE it was an investment. But, however odd it might sound, it was also a way for GE to connect to a small internet start-up that could teach the colossus something about how to develop and change in a new environment. Jack Welch, the legendary CEO of GE, wanted the whole company to start to think web, or, how the fast changing Net offered both threats and opportunities for GE.

In October 1999, Fondex became part of a management program that GE arranged as part of their training for senior and middle management. Basically, the idea of the program was that managers went out to the world to meet with new companies and business leaders, to discuss, learn and bring back their insights to GE at a campus get-together that Jack himself would attend. I was told that he wanted to be provoked by new ideas. That was the purpose of it all.

During that autumn we got a visit from four men in white shirts; one worked with car insurance at GE Capital, another with nuclear power plants, a third with gas turbines, and one of the managers traveled the world building a global insurance business within GE. What could I possibly teach these guys? Well, I started to present Fondex and our business. And after a while the unexpected happened. The men from General Electric were impressed.

And what impressed General Electric, one of the world's largest companies, was our size! We were so small. The meeting was held in our conference room with a glass wall towards the big open space that was Fondex's office. They had just realized that what they could see was actually the whole company. I pointed out the desk of the founder and CEO (me), the managing director for our Swedish operations, the finance officer, over there the marketing director, at the end of the room our editorial department, and there's the IT department, and so on. At GE they were used to each company having pretty much its own skyscraper. Here they could see the whole group in one room. It was obviously a new experience. They realized, quite visibly, that an internet company can be very small and still accomplish big things.

Fondex was the first internet fund supermarket in Sweden and a company that had slowly started to change the traditional and rigid fund market – an oligopoly dominated by banks – and it was forcing the larger players in that market to open up their fund distribution.

I too came to realize the power of the small company during our meeting. It doesn't take the resources of the largest company to be the most competitive company. It's all about your attitude to change and new ideas, how you respond to new opportunities and how well you can act on those ideas. In the fund market, Fondex was one of the first companies in Sweden to fully exploit opportunities on the internet. There was also the fact that over half the Swedish population invest in funds and are also savvy internet users. But it took the speed of a small company to do it. So Fondex's small size was its main asset. The big companies were too big to move fast enough.

The managers told me that Jack Welch had launched a new way of thinking in GE as a consequence of what they had learned when visiting various internet start-ups. In most of the important management positions at GE there was an additional boss, a shadow boss, whose only task was to challenge the existing business. They called it the 'destroy.your.business.com-manager,' a term that is now quite well known. But it came from GE and it indicates deep insight about how to run a business these days. To stay ahead you have to be prepared, at least mentally and often practically, to challenge what you do and what you know.

GE is still one of the best companies in the world, not because they're the biggest or one of the oldest, but because they have the ability to change. And they value the dynamics that exist, or should exist, between big and small companies.

66 Challenge your own business every day and pose questions about where you are going. Pose questions about where your world is going. (Maybe you are not going in the same direction, and if you're not you should be sure why.) To manage on the edge of chaos starts with the will to understand and the will to change. 99

What kind of manager are you, really?

Andy Grove, chairman of Intel, wrote a book that he called *Only the Paranoid Survive*. It's about how Intel has managed to thrive in the constantly changing computing industry where, sooner or later, something fundamental in your business world will change. He calls it a strategic inflection point, which occurs when change is so powerful that it fundamentally alters the way business is done. For chip-maker Intel it has happened many times. And I understand what he means. You can never relax.

66 SOONER OR LATER, SOMETHING FUNDAMENTAL IN YOUR BUSINESS WORLD WILL CHANGE 99

He was once interviewed by the *Financial Times* and talked about 'that creepy feeling' of something happening out there that you can't control and that might not only compete with you but might actually challenge the future of your whole business. I can identify with that too. We live in a world of ideas and the number of new ideas is growing exponentially, as each new idea is based on a new combination of old ideas and each new idea will give birth to an even newer idea. Why shouldn't there be someone out there with a better idea? Intel, as a big company, is vulnerable to new and better ideas that threaten to make the company irrelevant and redundant.

In the middle of the 1990s, Sun Microsystems challenged both Intel and Microsoft with its new idea: the network is the computer. The idea was that you do not need bulky computers with expensive hard disks with chips (from Intel) and software (from Microsoft). The power of the combined network is more than enough, connecting to its small, smart terminals.

Star Office is a company that develops office software, like word processing and spreadsheets, in direct competition with Microsoft. But Star Office's programs do not need to be installed on the hard disk, they run on the net and you log in to a website to use them in pretty much the same way that Hotmail or any other web-based e-mail service works. In August 1999, the company was bought by Sun who, to underline the idea about the network being the computer, communicated that they planned to supply the programs free on the internet. *Free*, as compared to some $400 for Microsoft Office.

When Sun bought Star, in a poetic-sounding acquisition, Sun's share price rose, but Microsoft's did as well, as they announced that they too were planning to release platform-independent office software that runs on the web. And Microsoft was believed to be in a reasonably good position to deliver. The new idea was certainly attractive to consumers, but it was not clear which company would eventually reap the profits. In 2000, Sun changed its message: that Sun is 'the dot in the dot com', meaning the centre of the action, I guess.

Established companies as well as newly launched start-ups must always decide if a new idea is a threat or an opportunity. The response can be to hire the person with the new idea or, as in the case above, buy the company that owns it. Or decide that the present world order will prevail and that the new idea does not have a future. Or launch an even newer idea that will compete. There are few, if any, companies that can afford not to care at all about new ideas.

The kind of manager you really are, or who you are as a person in general, is defined by your attitude towards new ideas. The internet was a new idea in Sweden around 1994–5. Most people didn't even notice it and among those who were aware of the new medium there was a line between those who thought it was a gadget that you didn't need to care much about, and those who saw both a future and a commercial value in it.

Investor, one of the flagships of Swedish industry, an investment company with large holdings in high profile companies such as ABB, Ericsson, SKF, Atlas-Copco and SEB, turned their noses up at the internet for a long time. In 1999, better late than never perhaps, they changed their mind and invested about $50 million in Spray, the Swedish web agency that was launched in 1995 and then developed into a European portal venture.

❝ THE NEW INTERNET MILLIONAIRES MARKED THEIR INDEPENDENCE BY LEISURE WEAR AND SNEAKERS AT BUSINESS MEETINGS ❞

At the press conference there was a clear distinction between those with and those without a tie. The dark suit and tie had become a symbol for those still working as office clerks, while the new internet millionaires marked their independence by leisure wear and sneakers at business meetings. Today, around the world, business leaders in traditional companies sometimes feel forced to pose without a tie and a suit in the press photographs they distribute to the media.

Just look at Jack Welch, the boss of GE, and Honeywell CEO Michael Bonsignore. Announcing GE's $45 billion acquisition of Honeywell in October 2000, they looked like they were off to play a cozy game of golf.

But an even more charming couple were media giant Bertelsmann's Thomas Middelhoff hugging Napster's Shawn Fanning in a spectacular deal between the Establishment and the Movement.

To change or not to change, that is the question

How should you look at change? In what kind of organization do you feel most at home? In the one that says *change the world!* (like Netscape), or, *change with the world!* (like Swedish telecom Telia), or, *don't change at all!* (like retailer H&M). These are of course not the companies' official slogans, but it's how I see them.

Netscape's contribution to changing the world was to launch the world's first browser on the internet which made the internet more accessible to users everywhere.

Telia first fought the internet and viewed it as a threat to the revenues it got from long-distance telephone calls, but later changed its mind to become a leading (and profitable) Internet Service Provider. Deutsche Telecom who started T-Online, and Spain's Telefonica with its Terra Networks, followed the same pattern.

The Swedish retailer H&M made some attempts to adjust to the internet but finally decided to stick to its traditional and successful strategy: to open real, physical shops in the best locations, like their fabulous store on Fifth Avenue in New York. Of course, H&M has got a a website, but the distribution is about the shops.

All these strategies are equally right, but different. In the same way, the managers behind those strategies are right, and different. How you view change and new opportunities defines your style of leadership.

Compare two different bosses at the Swedish car-maker Volvo: Pehr Gyllenhammar and Sören Gyll. Mr Gyllenhammar, CEO for 22 years between 1971 and 1993, experimented with the project he called Volvo and planned to build an oil pipeline to Norway one moment and to acquire a pharmaceutical company the next. Eventually, he had to go when his idea to merge Volvo with Renault became too much for the shareholders. His successor, Mr Gyll, on the other hand, spent his days deconstructing most of the fun things that Mr Gyllenhammar had dreamed up. To me, one was a business leader

"HOW YOU VIEW CHANGE AND NEW OPPORTUNITIES DEFINES YOUR STYLE OF LEADERSHIP"

who thought about the context in which he was working and the new ideas in this context, the other was a manager with short-term shareholder value as his only goal. Who was right? Well, they were different. But you have to understand what kind of leader you are.

On January 28 1999, Ford Motor Company bought Volvo for $6 billion. By then the new boss was Leif Johansson. The same week, internet portal Yahoo! bought GeoCities, a web community with about a hundred employees (and around a million regular users) for the same amount of money. Suddenly a website was valued at as much as the crown jewel of Swedish industry. Or was it the other way round? That Volvo, an old car-maker, could actually reach the same value as a leading, smart new-economy company. In any case, a website and a car company had basically the same market value. The idea of connecting people was worth as much as or more than transporting people in cars. A visionary business leader like Mr Gyllenhammar might have bought into Yahoo! in the mid-90s. Then Volvo might have been able to buy Ford instead in 1999!

Another case is the one of British retailers Tesco and Marks & Spencer. Tesco was one of the first traditional supermarkets to start a web business, in 1996. With TescoDirect the company today has a clear lead in the online grocery market. One of the success factors is that they base their operations around the existing network of stores, rather than building separate warehouses for their web operations (a strategy that was used by others in the US). But the main success factor is that they started early and never hesitated. One of its competitors, Marks & Spencer, has suffered at least partly because of its inability to make decisions in the web area. In one business magazine I read, an 'e-manager' at M&S said that the brand was strong and was associated with high customer loyalty – but I think they didn't dare risk this trust on the internet. Meanwhile, Tesco is reinforcing customer loyalty each time its customers log on to TescoDirect to buy groceries.

"Do this. The next time you read the newspaper, surf or watch TV – select a piece of news that means something to your industry. Then imagine that you have unlimited power. Would you change the company where you work, do nothing or quit your job to start a new company? How you are as a business leader is defined by how you respond to the outside world. **"**

To think in wholes and see it coming

Chaos is the concept of an unpredictable future – you don't know what will happen next. It's like the weather. Complexity, on the other hand, is the expression of a pattern with many variables where it can be difficult to understand how the parts are interrelated. Think about a computer or a large organization. In the same way that you can explain complexity if you learn how to understand the pattern, you can also predict the future by understanding the way chaos works. The secret lies in thinking in wholes.

I was a management consultant with SMG (Sifo Management Group), an international consultancy, in the middle of the 1990s. One of our customers, a telecom giant that had made a lot of money on telephone lines in a monopolistic market, was forced to redraw its map when the market was deregulated and a swarm of new competitors entered the market, while, at the same time, their customers were starting to use the internet to make long-distance calls for the cost of local calls. Seen from the telecom's traditional perspective, there was chaos. First reaction: panic. Next reaction: let's try to find new answers.

"YOU CAN PREDICT THE FUTURE BY UNDERSTANDING THE WAY CHAOS WORKS **"**

At SMG we worked with a model we called 'the Onion.' We used it to understand how the parts related to the whole. It looked like an onion cut in half, so you could see all the rings or layers. In our onion we used four layers:

one	Context (the first and outer layer)
two	Market
three	Company
four	Individual (the innermost part of the onion).

The first layer is the Context, which no one can change to any great extent. Here you find demographics, global economy, politics, media, technology, values and the greater macro environment where we all live and work.

The next layer is the Market where a company exists and does business. For example, for a car company this layer is about things like jeeps and four-wheel drives becoming popular family cars and tightening emissions regulations (usually as a consequence of developments in the Context).

In the third layer, the Company, we make strategies and plans depending on what happens in the Context and the Market. There are also companies, like Netscape in the 1990s or Ford in the 1920s, that can change or influence what happens in both the Market and the Context on their own. These companies usually become legends for playing a major part in an economic or historical shift. But for today's telecoms like British Telecom, Deutsche Telecom, France Telecom or Telia, for example, the last few years have mainly been about adapting to a new macro scenario. The better you adapt, the more competitive you will be.

At the Company level, decisions are made about how to respond to developments in the other layers, which will influence how to work, how to organize and which people to employ and educate in the inner layer, the Individual. The Individual is the smallest entity in this holistic approach, but probably the most important.

When Microsoft decided that they would be an internet company in 1995, they probably did an analysis like 'the Onion' (though I'm sure they didn't call it that). The internet was growing rapidly in the context, creating a demand for browsers from customers who were slowly starting to work and play in the

Market in new ways. This forced Microsoft to rethink its 'one PC on every table' strategy and launch a more connected internet strategy at Company level, which in turn led to acquisitions of web companies like Hotmail and Real Media to gain access to the right people (at the Individual level) with the right knowledge to be able to develop its own browsers and other internet products.

All this seems obvious, especially when you can look to the future and see what's coming. Have you ever had that feeling? But most companies can't see the future, or won't accept any future other than the 'official future' in their plans and strategies. They are victims of the chaos they experience when things are no longer what they used to be.

Take another consumer market, asset management and saving in funds. In Sweden, it started to change dramatically in the late 1990s.

Context: Subsidized PCs which had increased the PC-penetration rate in the households, together with inexpensive internet access and a population of early adopters, had made Sweden a country with one of the highest internet usage in the world. Interest rates continued to stay low and the stock market continued to go up, which stimulated investment. A new pension system was about to be launched that would further spur the growth of the fund market.

Market: Mutual fund (*UK: unit trust*) savings increased rapidly with assets under management approaching $100 billion in the beginning of 1999 in Sweden. Net inflow was high, the development dynamic. But the fund market itself was still rigid, a typical inefficient oligopoly with four large banks dominating around 85 percent of the assets, resulting in unsatisfactory transparency and a lack of open distribution channels. Meanwhile, more fund companies wanted to enter the lucrative Swedish market, especially the international fund management groups. The banks, wanting to keep the market for themselves, naturally tended to neglect them. In parallel, the fund market was getting increasingly more attention. It was developing into a real consumer market with extensive marketing and brand-building campaigns from fund companies, special editions about funds and stocks in the tabloids and TV shows about personal finance. And some of the five-million-plus retail fund investors (more than 60 percent of the population!), of whom many already used the internet for banking, started to ask why funds could not be just as easy on the internet. Added to the fact that funds are the perfect internet product – digital, without any need for physical distribution but with a giant need for correct information and search tools that the internet solves easily.

So, what do you think happened at Company level? An independent super-market for mutual funds with information and trading covering all funds was just a matter of time. It was pretty clear that the initiative wouldn't come from any of the established players in the market, who had optimized their staff, system, routines and distribution for the old market.

The Action room

'Action room' is my name for the space you have for exploiting new ideas in an organization. Even if companies and the individu-als in them can see the future, they'll find it hard to act on what they see. Our usual response is to close our eyes and hope the future will never come, or leave you alone.

Many companies are stuck with their old ideas. Without enough action room it's very difficult to gain any lead in fast-changing markets. Companies some-times decide that an old idea is the right idea and that it will prevail under new conditions. The established companies in the Swedish fund market, espe-cially the large banks, had very little action room as their businesses were based on selling their own set of funds through their own branches and thereby also subsidizing these branches. Changing this system was not an easy thing to do. The rest of the fund market with some 40 small or medium-sized companies sharing the remaining 15 percent of the market was too fragmented to make a move. So, we started Fondex and in May 1999 were the first to launch a fund supermarket in Sweden. It had some impact as a symbol of change and during the spring of 2000 the banks started to open up their channels for more funds.

And on the Individual level? Well, for Fondex it was all about recruiting a team that could build something that hadn't existed before. We employed fund specialists, engineers, journalists, marketing staff, and all the competencies that were needed to run a financial internet company. (I didn't know much about funds.)

You'll discover that this book moves freely in the four dimensions: Context → Market → Company → Individual. It swings between big and small questions, between global economy and project management, between the typography on a web page and Microsoft's internet strategies, what might occur in 10 years' time and what could happen the next second. Everything is interrelated and one thing leads to the other. I guess that, if nothing else, managers in the 21st century will have to broaden their scope significantly to look to the future every day.

       ❝ Do your own analysis. Don't take in too much information but make a rough sketch of the

Context, Market, and where your Company is in the whole thing. If you haven't done this exercise

before, you might be surprised by what you find. ❞

Order and chaos
There's a scene in Mel Brooks's Wild West satire *Blazing Saddles* where, in a saloon fight scene, the laconic Howard Johnson comments: 'Nietzsche said, out of chaos comes order.' And someone replies: 'Blow it out your ass, Howard.' It's funny because there's something pompous and ridiculous in using philosophers to comment on something ordinary. But I really *have* seen how the concepts of order and chaos apply to building a business.

Let's assume you are the CEO of a company with 500 employees, who, for whatever reason, use the internet for around an hour a day each. That equals around 125,000 hours of surfing a year. If an hour is worth, say, $100, the value of the surfing is $12.5 million. Would you consider that a cost/burden or an investment for the future?

The answer is: You don't know. That's what it's like working in an unpredictable environment. You don't know until afterwards whether the resources/ capital/ time/etc. spent were productive and produced a return, or if it was all just a waste. If you can confidently say that the 125,000 hours of surfing is a cost, you're probably quite narrow-minded. If you say it's an investment for the future you're naïve. The trick is to balance chaos and control.

In many companies, the goal is to achieve order and structure, and the chaos that sometimes reigns is disturbing and not welcome. Business managers tend to promote structure and fight disorder. Most management books are about creating organization, not disorganization. During my years in the internet industry I have also come to realize that business leaders in the new economy create a lot of chaos, but don't care much about the order.

Why live in order and chaos simultaneously? Order, structure and control are needed because the purpose of a company is to create an efficient platform for value creation and a machine for productivity. Furthermore, structure is needed to maintain rules and regulations, administrative routines, and everything else that has to do with the legal and practical context a company exists in.

❝ FOR MOST COMPANIES, THE UNEXPECTED IS THE MOST UNPLEASANT THING ❞

Chaos within this structure is where new ideas are born. Chaos without structure would be like a football game without rules – it wouldn't be creative, just a mess. Most artists know how important discipline is for the creation of new ideas. Total structure, though, will not create anything new. Structure is linear. Chaos has no direction at all, it tests everything, tears down everything, builds everything. Chaos is the uncontrollable power of the unexpected. For most companies, the unexpected is the most unpleasant thing. Organizations therefore rely on control, and the purpose of control is to counteract unwelcome surprises. The trick is to let chaos run free within controllable conditions.

At Icon Medialab, an internet consultancy where I worked for two years, I think that the management was quite aware of order and chaos (even if those precise words weren't used) and how to create the right mix between them. Of course, this was a new economy company that was founded in 1996, right in the chaos of the first internet wave. There were no rules for anyone.

The ultimate symbol of order, I believe, is the time-clock with its clocking-in cards. It is the machine that keeps track of when people come and go but it does not know or record what happens in between.

During one odd period of my life I was working as a civil servant at the Swedish Foreign Ministry and I had to clock in and clock out every day. It was the ultimate structured organization. Pretty soon I discovered that this clock provided the rhythm for the organization. No one really asked about the work I was doing, but the run-through of the time sheet was very important as this was the basis for overtime pay, an important source of extra income for underpaid bureaucrats. I don't know if some companies still use time-clocks, but it wouldn't surprise me if they did.

At Icon Medialab, there were no *fixed* working hours. Just a *lot* of working hours. When you arrived or left was of no great importance, the main thing was how you spent your time. As the time was spent on internet projects where consultants charged by the hour, this in turn meant that each hour spent on a project had to be carefully recorded in the time-reporting system, and later invoiced to the client. As in any consulting firm. A bureaucracy with a time-clock tends to be pure structure, whereas a consultancy without time-sheets is just chaos.

At Icon, order was removed where it was not needed and reinforced where it was relevant. Whether the staff worked day or night, Monday or Sunday didn't really matter. There can be chaos, and there was. But there was order governing the time you actually worked, creating a balance between order and chaos. And as the concept of overtime pay did not exist, I guess there was no need for a time-clock anyway.

Conditions like these tend to be complicated for senior managers in more established companies. They don't know where to loosen and where to tighten. So the result is often a tightening of control everywhere.

At the end of 2000 and in 2001, Icon Medialab and other high profile internet consultancies like Scient and Razorfish also had to practise the tightening of controls. As a result of the weaker financial market, dot com death and demands for profitability, they had to lay off people, refocus on big-enterprise clients, cut costs and bring in managers who represented Order, while getting rid of the ones who created the creative Chaos.

Rebels without a plan

A financial internet company like Fondex was quite a natural blend of order and chaos, because the company was born in order and chaos. The company existed in the context of a very tight framework of rules and regulations from the Swedish Financial Supervisory Authority that governed all financial activities in the company, like money handling and trading. But with regard to the website of the business, there were no rules at all. Of course, maintenance, support and security had to have the highest standards, but how new ideas for the website developed was a more chaotic process based on trial and error. You must be aware of what is order and what is chaos in your organization, where there is no room for error and where you can experiment freely. Many outstanding managers, like Jack Welch of GE, master the art of keeping a balance between the two.

In the music industry the feel for order and chaos comes naturally. When Amir and Rodde, producers/ singers of a fairly successful Swedish dance music band called Infinite Mass, were interviewed on ZTV, a cable channel, this is what they had to say about their business:

Q: How do you make a record?

A: There is no plan. We go into the studio and sometimes we record five new songs in a day, and other times none. You never know, it has to feel right.

Q: Are you planning to go international?

A: Yes, but you never know how it turns out. There's no book to follow.

Just one final example. In June 2000 I met with Jack Ma, a dynamic young Chinese who had recently launched Alibaba.com, a business-to-business internet venture. He explained the secret behind his success: 'I have no plan.' The explanation is that in a fast-changing environment there is no use for a plan, or even worse, plans can make you go in the wrong direction; and it's better to work than to plan. Of course, when Alibaba turned into a fairly large operation, plans were needed. Budgets, projects and international expansion all require plans, which investors and other parties are quite interested in, or like to see to feel a little more secure. And that's usually the purpose of a plan; it just has to be there.

66 Try making a list of what you regard as order and chaos in your own company. Then ask yourself what structures are actually needed, and which can be removed. Ask yourself where you can add in more creative disorder and anti-control. 99

To give change a name
One effect of the rapid development on the net, and in the economy in general, is that all of us working in it – from entrepreneurs, managers and accountants to politicians, analysts and journalists – must agree on what to call this mess.

If you can put a label on what's going on it's easier to understand it, and maybe it can even become a trend. It feels good to say 'Aha, now I understand where we're going,' only to have to turn around and change direction the next minute. It was like that in the digital media arena during most of the

1990s, a wonderful experiment in search of what worked and what was just a bubble. The 1990s are probably modern history's largest test lab for new technology, and most of it was tested on consumers who received new services and gadgets for free. We tested and we tried. Some things stayed, others went out the window. On the internet a new truth was launched every year, and the hype from the year before was dumped. That's the theme of the net: You raise something fast to the skies, then flush it down the drain with no sentimental feelings about it. There's always a new future.

The high tech industry is very enthusiastic. The world has also become more enthusiastic about new ideas. The markets of the world also have less patience with new ideas. As Jeff Bezos said in 2000 when the climate for dot coms was turning harder: 'Capital markets – they teach and they learn, last year they learnt, this year they teach.'

❝ THE SOUL OF THE NEW ECONOMY IS ALL ABOUT TESTING NEW THINGS ❞

However, today there is a capital infrastructure for new ideas, for making dreams come true. Sometimes they just stay dreams. The soul of the new economy is all about testing new things. This is how my 1990s look from a digital media perspective:

1993 Information highway (a concept that became famous thanks to US Vice-President Al Gore)

1994 Multimedia (could mean just about anything, usually the convergence of just about everything)

1995 World wide web (the net as a digital brochure)

1996 Intranets (aha, maybe it can be useful as an internal communication tool)

1997 Push (the internet is actually the mass medium of the 21st century where we push content to the user ... remember Pointcast?)

1998 Portals (it's about traffic, the user shall come to you)

1999 1st quarter: Destinations (the portals were just an entrance)

1999 2nd quarter: Infomediaries (destinations as a vertical portal ...)

1999   3rd quarter: Free internet access providers

1999   4th quarter: B2B (we don't make any money on consumer services)

2000   The beginning: Traditional media merge with new media

2000, The rest of the year: Dot com death and P2P (the venture capitalist to the entrepreneur: 'Show me the path to profitability'). P2P was also the new catchphrase for companies like Napster, based on file-sharing, or peer-to-peer services

This lust for experimentation has in turn stimulated a faith in the future and a feeling that everything is possible. Sometimes you have to reconsider and re-learn. In 2000, some suggested that B2C (Business to Consumer services) actually meant Back to College; go read your old financial textbooks and refresh your mind about the relationship between costs and revenue.

But rules are there to be broken. The chaotic market that characterized the environment of the companies we made heroes – Amazon, Netscape, AOL – actually legitimized them as companies in a new economy. If you live in chaotic times, then chaotic or strange strategies are right. There is no handbook. You have to write it yourself. And many of the thousands of analysts that are trying to evaluate the companies should not feel stupid. How can they understand what's happening if the companies themselves don't fully understand? Anyone trying to make serious predictions about the future is a fool, especially if it concerns the stock market. However, when profits became the new catchphrase in 2000 it made analysts relax. That concept was really easy to understand!

When you start a company or launch a new ground-breaking project, you never know *exactly* what you are doing. The restless feeling that it must be right drives you. But one thing you have to do quickly is to find a name for whatever it is you're doing. A project, a company, a venture of any kind will remain abstract until it has a name. People are like that, we want a name for everything. And it has to be the right one, showing the right idea. Icon was one of the new web agencies, but not to limit it too much the founders called it 'Icon Medialab.' Spray chose the name 'Interactive Media Agency,' Adera, an advertising agency that changed into an internet consultancy decided they were an 'e-agency.' The main thing is not to be a boring 'consultant.'

> "You don't get many chances to present yourself or what it is that your company does. So, ask yourself: What is your company? What is your market? Who are you? As a business leader you are also responsible for labeling the context in which you exist. And that's actually a way of influencing the context itself. Play around with some concepts. It's fun."

The CEO as DJ

The role of the manager is changing. The archetype for the manager in the 1900s is Alfred P. Sloan Jr, the late legendary CEO for General Motors. He became a world famous business leader for a giant with over 600,000 employees and an organization that symbolized both success and a monster of bureaucracy.

But his predecessor William Durant, the founder, was probably more of the typical business leader for the beginning of the 2000s. He founded General Motors in 1908 and then went about acquiring and starting companies like crazy, building new cars and testing ideas to profit from the new opportunities in the early days of the automobile industry, a market as promising as the internet in the 1990s. He had no plan, other than the vision in his restless mind.

Eventually, in 1920, Alfred P. Sloan Jr took over from William Durant to clean up the conglomerate, establishing policy-making committees, drawing charts and writing plans. This balance between creative chaos and the organized structure laid the foundation for the modern GM.

Chaos and order represent two very different kinds of managers. The challenge for today's manager is to represent both, and to find the balance between chaos and order, within oneself and in the organization.

Success is created in the mix. Good managers today have a talent for mixing: mixing between innovation and control, between the greater vision and attention to detail in execution; mixing start-ups with established business; mixing new services around a brand; mixing ideas, but also mixing competencies and putting together dynamic teams of people.

A good business leader is like a DJ. Sometimes he looks out over the dance floor and lets himself be influenced by what he sees out there, in the market and the ever-changing world. Sometimes he changes the mix, turns up the volume and tries some new tracks to heat up the floor. It's interplay and you have to have an open mind.

Commercial activity and business is about order, and likewise chaos must build on structure; otherwise it will just be a mess. A DJ mixes around a steady beat. In a company, that beat is its vision, its business idea and its culture. A nightclub is, for me, a great metaphor for a company. It is dynamic, everything can happen, it's controlled, yet somewhat out of control, but in the background there is a rhythm of pumping base guiding all activities. At an internet company, for example, there is usually a constant mixing and testing of ideas and influences around the beat that is the vision or the culture in the company. Unlike a nightclub that closes in the morning, the mix should never end in a company.

> **“UNLIKE A NIGHTCLUB THAT CLOSES IN THE MORNING, THE MIX SHOULD NEVER END IN A COMPANY.”**

Richard Branson is a great DJ. For over twenty years he has been mixing new tunes around the Virgin beat and built a £5 billion-a-year group with over 220 companies and 25,000 employees. He is the master of the eternal start-up. He has described business as a 'fluid, changing substance – a company that never stands still.'

Stelios Haji-Ioannou knows how to mix to a steady beat. His EasyGroup, founded in 1998, includes easyJet, the discount airline, easyRentacar, an online rental service, easyValue, a price comparison web site, easyMoney, online financial services, and easyEverything – a chain of the world's largest internet cafès. This is an example of a new company that grew fast with a DJ who saw the opportunities on the dance floor – like the deregulation of the European airline industry and the rapid spread of the internet – and created a formidable groove in his nightclub. The bottom line beat is an unbeatable value for the customers.

Akio Morita was born in 1921 and founded Sony in 1946. He launched the first Japanese tape recorder in 1950, the world's first all-transistor television in 1960 and the first home video tape recorder in 1965. It was the first Japanese firm to be listed on the New York Stock Exchange, in 1970. When Sony released the Walkman in the late 1970s, Akio Morita said: 'We don't believe in market research for a new product unknown to the public. So we never do any.' He used intuition and his feel for the Sony rhythm. In his company, he was also mixing different management concepts, like Japanese and Western, which is another characteristic of a great CEO-DJ.

With revenues of around $1 billion, some 150 million registered users (and just some 3000 employees), Yahoo! is one of the world's largest internet companies. In 1993, Jerry Yang and David Filo put together 'Jerry's Guide to the Internet,' which later become Yahoo! Since then they have been mixing new services around a brand that stands for making more use of the internet. The first years were about helping people find information. Free e-mail and chat came in 1997, followed by e-commerce and recently mobile services and streaming video were added to the vast amount of content. Furthermore, Yahoo! adapts its content to local markets and its users around the globe log on to services like 'Yahoo! Finance,' 'Yahoo! Weather' and 'Yahoo! Shopping.'

Amazon.com might have been mixing too much with its business. The virtual bookseller turned books-video-music merchant now wants to sell everything from lawn mowers to antiques to everybody everywhere on the net. The larger the mix, the larger the cost of the venture and the larger is the risk that you will lose the clarity of the brand. Jeff Bezos, Amazon's founder, would probably argue that the brand stands for outstanding customer service (just as Volvo stands for safety and Gucci stands for luxury). If you are going to be a DJ, you need the rhythm of a powerful beat.

I met Amazon's Jeff Bezos briefly in Stockholm in the autumn of 2000. It was a very interesting experience. He did a presentation with no slides, numbers, graphs or written text. It was just Jeff and a message: We are going to create the world's greatest customer experience. And you believed him, because this was probably the most enthusiastic guy you had ever seen or met. You thought that if the whole company culture was like him, Amazon was probably going to make it. He had surely created a groove in his nightclub.

Porsche is one of the most admired brands in the world. They also have a clear picture of what they are doing. Around their brand they carefully mix new models – the Carrera, the Boxter and the Cayenne – never losing the feel for the bottom line beat. This is how they describe their philosophy: 'The future for Porsche has never been a journey of uncertainty. The route has been determined by the company's clear, yet flexible, sense of direction. Porsche's traditional and modern values will continue to be relevant in the future. The very nature of our products means that emotion plays a central role in our vision. Porsche is inextricably linked with the concept of taking control. Our business meets its challenges head-on. Driving the future, in every possible sense.'

Never forget the beat. In an increasingly chaotic business community, a clear and focused identity will be increasingly important. Nobody can afford to be unclear and unfocused in a super fast and turbulent market. You've got to steer. The first lesson in the new economy is to lead and manage, not mismanage and create more chaos. The CEO-DJ has a natural feel for how to manage his dance floor and, remember, as a business leader it is always you who picks the tunes.

❝ THE CEO-DJ HAS A NATURAL FEEL FOR HOW TO MANAGE HIS DANCE FLOOR AND, REMEMBER, AS A BUSINESS LEADER IT IS ALWAYS YOU WHO PICKS THE TUNES ❞

CHAPTER TWO

Action: To start up and re-start

I FEEL LIKE IF YOU HAVE AN IDEA,

YOU JUST GOTTA DO IT.

CRAIG KANARICK, CO-FOUNDER RAZORFISH

The start-ups and the re-starters

I subscribe to many newsletters and magazines, maybe too many. Magazines like *Business 2.0, FastCompany*, and *Wired* each call themselves 'a new business magazine for the new economy.' I would call them, and all the other similar publications, 'the chronicles of the start-ups and the re-starters.' They provide biographies of companies that never existed before, based on ideas that never existed before. They are also about companies that have existed for a long time, which are embarking on journeys of change as they start all over again, or at least want to give the impression that they are changing. I think that only these two kinds of companies can succeed – the start-ups and the re-starts.

Read the full-page ads in any issue of *Business 2.0, FastCompany* or *Wired*, and you have an impressive list of start-ups accompanied by more or less powerful ideas: Webmiles.com: *Any airline, any flight, any time.* Brightware: *eCustomer assistance made simple.* Expercity.com: *A human behind every click.* AuctionWatch.com: *Buy anywhere, sell anywhere, start here.* Commerce One: *Many markets, one source.* LivePerson: *Give your site a pulse.*

Many of the companies you saw in the ads do not exist any more. They represented the future, but did not have a future themselves. Old companies also want to build a future. That's why old companies initiate change in their organizations, launch new projects and start again. They become re-starters.

The message from McKinsey, one of the world's oldest and most respected management consultancies, is that every generation has its equation, in this case, $e=mc^k$. I guess that is the sign of a re-starter. In a fun e-mail that went around I also saw $e=mc^2$, meaning 'in e-business you end up paying twice as much for management consultants than you had budgeted for.'

And then you have Microsoft: *Where do you want to go today*? Before, the message was to go to Microsoft, now it's about enabling people to go anywhere.

One of the busiest advertisers on the back cover of leading new economy magazines is Absolut Vodka, *produced at the famous old distilleries near Åhus in accordance with more than 400 years of Swedish tradition*, as it says on the label of the bottle.

Usually, old companies brag about their history, while new companies are ashamed of theirs. In the new company there are no profits to show, no 100 years' anniversary books to write, no museums to build. The only thing they have is the future, and the only thing that the new company wants to prove is that it was right about the future and that it owns this future. Or, rather, to show that it could influence and make a difference in this future. This is why, I think, we start our companies. Any reason, however, is good. The point is not why you start, but simply to start. Action is always more valuable than talk.

> 66 USUALLY, OLD COMPANIES BRAG ABOUT THEIR HISTORY, WHILE NEW COMPANIES ARE ASHAMED OF THEIRS 99

To learn, unlearn and relearn

IKEA, the global furniture retailer, is a re-starter. Their stores draw huge crowds of visitors and they hardly need the net to be successful, but it is possible that they might be even more successful if they can transfer their knowledge from the physical world to the virtual and reach their customers in new ways. In 2000 they launched their new website that offered around 700 of their total of 10,000–12,000 products, in what could be seen as a giant experiment in re-starting.

General Motors is a re-starter. With sales of around $180 billion and close to 400,000 employees they are the world's largest industrial corporation. Like many other giant corporations, such as Boeing and General Electric, GM has its own internet-based B2B exchange for suppliers. Furthermore, they adopted a very open approach (a key element of web thinking) and formed an industry-wide exchange together with Ford and DaimlerChrysler. When competition turns into cooperation, it's usually a sign that old companies are becoming re-starters with controversial strategies that will create more value in the long run.

In 1998, GM launched BuyPower.com, its website for auto e-shopping. And one of the individual brands in the group, Oldsmobile, has proved itself a re-starter with the most visited website in the group. According to one survey, one-third of new car buyers visited the website before buying. Oldsmobile has renewed its brand on the net and has managed to reach new customers by smart integration of interactive and broadcast media.

Time will tell whether GM is a successful re-starter and whether they can realize their vision of making the car a rolling portal. In any case, web thinking will be changing the culture in the company as GM is forced to think more like a small company.

It is a myth that only people like internet entrepreneurs and new media visionaries create the future. Many work in silence while creating great changes. That is really what the big change in society is all about – the re-starters. A true shift in an economy happens when the masses change their behavior, not when the 10 percent called early adopters move to a new gadget. So, keep an eye on all those who actually represent the old, and when they turn to the new. Like the futurist Alvin Toffler said: 'The illiterate of the 21st century will not be those who cannot read and write, but those who cannot learn, unlearn, and relearn.'

"THE ILLITERATE OF THE 21ST CENTURY WILL NOT BE THOSE WHO CANNOT READ AND WRITE, BUT THOSE WHO CANNOT LEARN, UNLEARN, AND RELEARN"

Building without knowing

So far, much in the new economy has been about building with a goal – but building without completely knowing. The drive behind the projects of change is usually a feeling of being right, that this must be the way, that there are fantastic opportunities to take advantage of.

The new economy is not based on thorough market surveys. Most leaders today understand that you have to take risks to succeed. But not only that. You have to take steps into the unknown, which is something more scary than calculated risks. When German telecom operators bid €50 billion for the licenses to third-generation mobile networks, it's more than a risk. It's a big bet. However, not many companies would bet on the alternative.

It might seem like the new economy is all about money and economics. Well, it's not. It's about building new things, participating in the opportunities of a global market (and the local market) and being pioneers in a new era. It has been said that it is state of mind. I agree. The very economics of the new economy is actually nothing exciting at all, it's just like economics have always been: allocating scarce resources, and keeping track of the outcome in a profit and loss statement and a balance sheet.

Working in the new economy is essentially about working in a knowledge society where the main asset is what we learn from doing business in new-ways in new markets. When the share prices of new-economy companies drop, the knowledge and the experience remains. That is the real value, in the long term.

The paradox of being 'safe'

When people leave old companies to form new ones, they realize that they have to take risks to achieve safety. If you're not taking a personal risk, it means that you are betting on the status quo, or letting somebody else decide your future, which might be dangerous in times of fast change. What was considered the safest option for an individual – secure employment in a big corporation – is now turning into a hazard as both the context and the big corporations are in constant flux. The only way, therefore, to be safe is to take personal risks to stay one step ahead of the chaos. This is the modern paradox: if you are aiming for security, you will be at risk – if you are willing to take risks, you will probably be safe.

The web became a catalyst for entrepreneurship. Internet = opportunities. The net provided a vehicle for realizing ideas and made people think about ideas. They thought: 'Why not try this?' Well, why not? Others have done it. Why not me? It's the same process of thought regardless of whether it concerns the individual or the big company. Before, the answer to the question was probably 'not.' Today the answer is more likely 'just do it.' What do you have to lose? But if you don't do it, you probably *will* lose.

Let's hope that the downturn in the dot com market that started in 2000 will not discourage entrepreneurs whose companies have been shut down, sold, restructured, or gone bankrupt. Failures must also be seen as something valuable, something to learn from in order to make things better next time. Unfortunately, Europe, unlike the US, has a tradition of looking down on failed entrepreneurs and businesses. We must build a second-chance culture. Also, let's hope that crashed dot coms don't give the big companies the impression that the small companies were wrong, and the old-timers were right. The industry has changed for good.

Nobody cares about change, except you

Amidst all this talk of change, you must remember that nobody is interested in change. Nobody, except you, is interested in your idea coming true. Most people will be negative, doubting, questioning, indifferent, and even fighting against you or just showing a lack of time and interest. That's what it's like to start a thing that otherwise wouldn't exist. But it's enough that only one person – you – believes, and the miracle will happen. The thing will start anyway.

66 NOBODY, EXCEPT YOU, IS INTERESTED IN YOUR IDEA COMING TRUE 99

The world's first management guru, Niccolo Machiavelli who lived in Florence during the Renaissance, put it this way in his leadership handbook, *The Prince*:

IT MUST BE CONSIDERED THAT there is nothing more difficult to carry out, nor more doubtful of success, nor more dangerous to handle, than to initiate a new order of things. For the reformer has enemies in all those who profit by the old order, and only lukewarm defenders in those who would profit by the new order.

Oh, how I experienced this when I started Fondex. We had counted on all the smaller fund companies joining our new marketplace for mutual funds on the internet. But it turned out they were, well, lukewarm. And of course we had enemies in all the big banks that profited heavily from the old order. We asked if we could sell their funds through Fondex. They said no. We started to sell their products anyway.

" Never ask for permission to start a new thing. If you ask others and ask what they think, or you need others to get you started, the answer will usually be no. It 's about having enough drive to start anyway. Don't ask. Start! "

In the beginning there was an idea

All start-ups and re-starters start with the idea. Let's try it. Usually, new ideas conflict with the old ones. That is natural in the ideas economy. There is also conflict between the right and wrong ideas. And you never know which ideas are the right ones and which are wrong.

I read an interview with the author J.K. Rowling in *Newsweek*. This is how she described how she got her idea for Harry Potter in 1990 on the train between London and Manchester:

AND I HAD THIS PHYSICAL REACTION to it, this huge rush of adrenaline, which is always a sign that you've had a good idea, when you've a physical response, this massive rush ... I'd had ideas that I liked, but never quite so powerful. And Harry came first, in this huge rush. Doesn't know he's a wizard ...

Her vision of the teenage wizard was so strong that she could feel it in her whole body. Have you ever had that sensation, when the idea feels so great that your body shivers? Then every time you think about the idea again, it makes you warm and it feels good. But it might not be so easy to translate that feeling into words and to communicate it to others who don't get that same great feeling about your idea.

Furthermore, a good idea must be able to change the behavior of its users, like checking your e-mail on the web (Hotmail) or sending text messages over your mobile telephone (SMS). Another measure, I think, is how simple and appealing an idea is. Try this: 'Harry Potter teenage wizard.' It's just great.

Both start-ups and re-starters must have strong and original ideas to succeed. The difference is that the start-up starts with nothing more than the idea; no organization and no other resources. The re-starter starts with an old idea that it has to get rid of, before launching the new, better idea.

66 You should have your own measure of a good idea. Actually, the best test is not an intellectual or mental one, but rather a 'physical' test. It should **feel** right. 99

Growth = ideas + resources + action

There's a lot of talk. There's a lot of money. There's a lot of will. There are a lot of good wishes. But real value is made through action. The real value is created by the ones building companies and organizations, infrastructure and customer bases, products and services, the ones making the new economy work day and night – and this is done at detail level: coding java scripts and xml-pages, calling customers and cleaning up in the kitchen.

Like any increase in the GDP or in living standards, we have the workers to thank for it – the ones laying down the rails in the new infrastructure. My kind of working-class hero is the webmaster or the programmer. The one who makes it work. Companies, organizations and movements are built with hard work and the tedious day-to-day struggle with small things. History has shown that the future belongs to the ones who deliver.

All new things, like a start-up, or a new project in an old company, start with an idea and a vision of change, but nothing can ever be built on ideas alone. Growth is the result of the formula: ideas + resources + action. One of these variables without the others makes no sense.

Think about big banks' or major airlines' global advertising. So many resources and so much action, but nothing to see but old and dull ideas. Think about the young entrepreneur without venture capital, all action and ideas (sometimes it's enough). But no resources. Think about the political system, usually, with all the ideas and the resources, but not much action.

Then again, think about Richard Branson who has proved to be a master at combining ideas and resources with a lot of action. And, well, maybe except for the balloon trips, the action has produced a lot of economic growth. Of course, ideas + resources + action can also produce a waste of capital.

The platform where ideas, resources and action are combined is usually the legal entity called a company. That is why I see the company as a vehicle for new ideas.

In the center of the action stands the Doer. This is the person who creates change and makes a difference. Without him or her there would be no drama, no change, no fun, and no new economy to write history books about. This person can be a start-up entrepreneur or someone in the old company. Doers are needed everywhere and they exist everywhere. Doers need a vehicle in which to put their idea and drive away.

Moving at the speed of vision
Small companies usually have a higher market value relative to their size because they are expected to grow faster than larger, more mature companies. (This is true in a bull market, anyway; in a recession it might be the opposite.)

Big companies grow more slowly, not only because they are already big but because they contain so many people who also have to change to grow. The big company will usually develop more slowly because it moves at the rate of the lowest common denominator in the company. Everybody's got to be on board before the ship can sail.

The small company, on the other hand, develops at the speed of the highest common denominator, which is usually the shared vision to change the world. Everybody in the small company runs in the same direction, and acts on the same agenda. There is no history, only a future. The company moves with the speed of getting more people on board. Or, call it moving at the speed of vision.

It's not unusual that the small company picks the best talent from the bigger companies and rewards them with stock options with the potential to rise rapidly in value as the company grows. The market value of small companies usually increases faster than that of the bigger company, since the small company starts from such a low level. But, on the other hand, there is a huge risk that the small company will never reach any higher valuations or that it might go bankrupt. Therefore small companies have to compete with the big in paying market-level salaries to top executives who are not interested in risky options.

While big companies can be said to be handicapped by their sheer size and their history, small companies have a kind of social responsibility to help the big ones. That usually means that the big guy buys the small one to get access to people, technology or just the right culture. It's a sort of modern welfare business politics, based on capitalism. This is an interesting dynamic between the Establishment and the Movement.

'Launch a website and change the world'

A small company can accomplish more than ever before as a result of the huge opportunities that have emerged thanks to the network economy, which can make a new idea break through with exponential power in an ongoing paradigm shift.

Just take Napster, the website for sharing music files. The company and its 19-year-old founder Shawn Fanning were sued by the record industry for intellectual property infringement as millions of teenagers used their software to download Metallica and other artists. Is this a criminal company or just a symbol of a paradigm shift?

Creating big things with a small company might seem simple and that is also why start-ups are so attractive. 'Launch a web site and change the world.' In practice, it is extremely difficult to do. A company with just 10 employees can indeed accomplish as much as a company with 10,000, but you must have:

- the right idea

- with the right timing

- in the right context

- with the right team of people to do it.

You can add a favorable and strong capital market with a long-term view to that. You can also add understanding and favorable customers. Some companies might not know that they have the right idea, at the right time, in the right place, with the right team when they start. They might have a clue, but do not know how right they are. One example: David Filo and Jerry Yang, who started Yahoo! in 1994, have described their company's progress like this: It started with an idea that became a hobby and grew into a full-time passion. They never said: First we wrote a business plan, then we built a global group. It was about having fun all the way (and a great deal of luck).

The Foundation

Instead of the traditional business plan, especially at the beginning of a project, I usually think in terms of what I call the Foundation of the business – the reason for its existence. This is the intellectual manifestation of the idea. It can be described as a deep understanding of the idea, the business, revenue drivers, key challenges and how to succeed.

By understanding the Foundation of the business, you will also be much better at explaining it to investors and other interested parties. What does the foundation contain? (Or, if you wish, you can simply call it a business memo.)

- the idea in short words – ideally just one sentence
- the people behind it, and the organization
- the context and the market where the idea is to be realized
- the business model – how the company makes money
- the growth engine – how the company plans to expand
- a practical description of the customer and the needs the idea solves (or creates)
- a financial example, with numbers for initial investment and costs to run it.

Ideally, you fit this on maximum five pages. If you get the foundation right, you can be much more certain if and how you go ahead with the project. You don't need to plan so much but can be more flexible as you go. On the other hand, if the foundation is wrong, no plan in the world can help you. You need a new foundation.

Let the foundation take its time to develop; the more robust it is, the faster you can move when the company gets going. In Fondex, we worked for over a year to get our foundation right. The foundation is also the foundation for the business plan, which could be called the complete picture.

66 Never plan more than is absolutely necessary. The mistake many companies make is to plan too much, without reviewing the plans often enough. It is better to act. (In due time there will be plans, be sure of that.) 99

The business plan – a story about the future

Regardless of whether you are a start-up or a re-starter, your business plan is your story about the future. Once you have all the fundamentals in the foundation, the business plan is the storyboard.

You tell a story about your business and what is going to happen. What the outcome will be. And what it will cost. Anyone who listens to the story will judge it as you do when you watch a film or read a book; you like some things, others suck, but afterwards you're left with a feeling of the whole. It depends on the different parts and how they interrelate. If it's a good story it will highlight what is new and exciting.

66 THE
BUSINESS PLAN
IS A STORY
ABOUT THE
FUTURE, AND IT
MUST BE ALIVE
AT ALL
TIMES 99

A business plan is important for any entrepreneur looking for venture capital – the idea on paper is the only thing you have – but it should be just as natural for existing companies. The business plan is a story about the future, and it must be alive at all times. In reality, it's even more important for later stages in a company when the business and the budget grows.

Fondex had no detailed plan in the beginning, except for a vision and a slide pack of PowerPoint pictures: our Foundation. The company was based on an idea, and a team of Doers. We had a story about the future, but hardly a plan. And there was no need for a plan. We had 'to do' lists instead.

When Fondex's business started to expand, the need grew for a steering document with strategies, goals, schedules, a budget, and a presentation of where the company was heading. That was when we wrote the business plan. The business plan became a living organism within the company – reviewed, and usually rewritten, at least every three months.

Also, when Fondex became part of the UK internet group Moneyextra, we planned more because the organization grew and there were more layers of decision-makers who needed words and numbers.

Internet time and calendar time

You sometimes hear that one calendar year is equal to four internet years. In a way, it is true. In practice, it means that if you are going to do something in 'three months' this is really three weeks in the fast company. Time is divided by four. I'm sometimes shocked when I realize how little real time has actually passed and how much has been accomplished in that time. The first year of building Fondex felt, physically and mentally, like four years in my body and mind, and I often have to remind myself that it was just one calendar year.

LifeMinders Inc., an example of action and planning that was highlighted by *Fast Company* magazine, is an organization that has adopted what it calls the three-week project deadline. If it can't be done in three weeks, don't do it. The big idea you want to come true is dependent on many small actions and opinions. It is better to get things done and compromise in order to achieve your three-week deadline than to try to achieve too much and have an ever-expanding deadline. If you have big projects, break it down to three-week units. Small

❝ IF IT CAN'T BE DONE IN THREE WEEKS, DON'T DO IT ❞

companies are usually good at thinking in terms of big visions, and realizing them with small solutions. Big companies usually mean big (costly, lengthy, complicated, all-at-once) solutions.

Everything is, indeed, relative. That is why change in a small, fast-growing company is often perceived as something much more dramatic than change in a big, established organization. Sure, changes can be dramatic in big organizations, but for the small company, employing one more person can mean staff growing by 100 percent in one day! Now, *that's* the everyday drama of the little company!

This is especially the case in a fast-growing (or falling) market like the internet industry where development can be chaotic and unpredictable. A small company can go through as much in three months as a large or traditional company experiences in several years. In just one quarter, the small company can see the arrival of three new competitors, the bankruptcy of another, it can complete two rounds of financing, increase its staff by 1000 percent and increase 10 times in value, or sometimes lose all its value.

In this environment, the traditional one-year business plan won't do. In 2000, Fondex re-wrote its business plan more than four times because of changes in the market and the outside world. You might just as well make it a routine to re-write the business plan every quarter, but in your mind you're revising it every day and questioning its underlying assumptions.

The planning process in a fast company looks something like this:

- management meeting once every week, evaluation of current plans and operations
- full-day strategic workshop once a month to evaluate the business, review the results and key figures, and take a broader view of things
- updated business plan quarterly
- and, of course, daily meetings in the kitchen.

Maybe you can't compare politics with business, but maybe you can. Politics may also involve plans, but it certainly moves at a different speed. The Swedish Social Democratic Party presented a new party manifesto in 2000. Traditionally, they have re-written the mission statement every 15 years to keep up with the changing world. The last time they did it was in 1990, so the text that was presented in 2000 signaled a new beat. As the world was moving faster, they had decided to re-write the party manifesto every 10 years instead!

To play a new mix around a bottom-line beat

The business plan must be a living tale about the future. Usually, it doesn't mean changing the vision or the business idea. No, the idea behind the business, or the Foundation, is the beat around which the business evolves. Changing the business plan is merely like playing a new mix to that bottom-line beat. An ever-evolving business plan is part of the culture in a growing company. The business plan is not a document in a binder on the shelf in the CEO's office.

In a start-up, your natural mental state is to work with high speed (even though I have learned that you are never in the hurry you think you are). For the manager who wants to turn a company into a re-starter, planning is the place to start. Stop breathing to the rhythm of the one-year plan and start living in three-month intervals instead. And plan in less detail.

As each business is unique, or should be, and the people running the business constitute a unique set of individuals in one way or another, and the company in its context is a unique company, with its own products and services, doing its own thing, it follows that the business plan, also, is probably unique. Accordingly, there is no ready-made handbook for any given company. You might pick up some advice along the way, but in the end you must always write your own handbook. This is how Richard Branson put it in his book *Losing My Virginity*:

❝THERE IS NO READY-MADE HANDBOOK FOR ANY GIVEN COMPANY. YOU MIGHT PICK UP SOME ADVICE ALONG THE WAY, BUT IN THE END YOU MUST ALWAYS WRITE YOUR OWN HANDBOOK❞

TO BE SUCCESSFUL, YOU HAVE TO be out there, you have to hit the ground running, and if you have a good team around you and more than your fair share of luck you might make something happen. But you certainly can't guarantee it just by following someone else's formula.

66 Read a lot, surf around, meet people, listen, try, fail, take some advice. But never forget that you have to write the handbook for your company yourself. No other management handbook than your own will ultimately fit your business. 99

It's smart to be slow

66 SPEED IS ONE OF OUR ERA'S MOST VALUED COMPETITIVE FACTORS, AND A MEASURE OF SUCCESS 99

In Silicon Valley there is an expression: 'Speed is God, Time is the Devil.' Basically, it means that the faster you get your company or new product on the market, the better. Speed is one of our era's most valued competitive factors, and a measure of success. A company is dependent on its ability to launch faster, employ faster, develop new products faster, sell faster. Some even say that it's irrelevant to talk about rich and poor countries, it's really about fast and slow ones.

Speed can also be a trap. I have seen this in at least three different ways. First, the need for speed can be an illusion. It's not unusual that the speed in a start-up is demanded by the entrepreneurs (driven by their vision, and scared of competition), venture capitalists (worried about their investment), and just about any other involved party – everybody except the customers. It's rare that consumers demand that a new service, like some bright mobile internet application, is launched *now*. No, in reality, the customer does not care when they get the new product or service, now or next year. They are usually fine as they are. Take Boo.com, the web-based sports-gear retailer, as an example. They were able to build a global organization with hundreds of employees in a short time, and shut it down just as quickly. The majority of potential customers probably hardly even notice that the company ever existed. If start-ups moved with the speed of their customers, they would move slower. You are rarely in as much of a hurry as you think you are.

Second, there is another expression regarding speed. It might be used in Silicon Valley, but it is actually from the art and practice of negotiation: *The first mover is the first loser*. If you make a move early you expose yourself.

Finally, high speed usually equals high risk. You also have to be aware that speed costs, since it requires a lot of resources. Some say that you need to be fast to survive. That's rubbish. The speed can just as easily kill you, and has killed many companies that tried to grow too fast. Grow organically if you can. Pause sometimes and ask yourself: Why the hurry? If you think deeply about it you might find that there is no hurry at all.

- If you're smart you move with the speed of the customers and end-users of your service. Not with the speed of hype. The world's most prominent companies have grown organically. Just look at IKEA, for example.

- It's not so smart to spend a lot of money just to let others learn from you. Sometimes you have to resist the temptation to be first. Let others lead the way, and outsmart them.

- Speed thrills and speed kills. Ask yourself if it's worth the risk.

A friend of mine, Soki Choi, has made a distinction between fast and smart companies. She is the founder and CEO of Bluefactory, a company in a very fast and dynamic market: wireless internet. They develop mobile games, games you can download and play on your mobile phone. Bluefactory could probably be terribly fast, but they have decided to be smart instead. For example, instead of developing cool games for third-generation wireless infrastructure, they develop content that works on today's technology like text messaging and WAP. They focus on profitability now, rather than gambling for profitability tomorrow (and are proud about the low burn-rate).

They don't rush into hyper expansion in new geographical markets. They focus on the home market. They keep a low profile, because not bragging about your plans before you have implemented them gives you respect in the industry. They think long term. They work hard, they work fast, and they work smart. I like them because they are a 'slow' company, and in the long term they will outrun anybody.

Basic speed

Having said it can be smart to be slow and that speed can kill you, it must also be said that speed is essential for a company. It should be a natural, basic speed that reflects the tempo in the company. Normally, it's just a matter of being practical.

You should always be as fast as possible. To act with basic speed is usually about three things:

- creating focus and not straying from the main task
- doing the right things in the right order
- simplifying rather than making things complicated.

Sticking to the plan

Speed, at the most basic level, is also about drawing up time plans and keeping to them. If, for example, you are going to launch a new electronic order system in eight months, you have to start a series of sub-plans immediately, from the various technical sub-projects to marketing.

It is strange how the whole economy actually boils down to a myriad of companies busy drawing plans and then trying to stick to them.

How do you draw up a time plan? Well, there are a number of ways and I won't go into them here. The point is that making plans is the same as getting commitments. You start by gathering all parties involved in the project, such

> ❝ THE WHOLE ECONOMY ACTUALLY BOILS DOWN TO A MYRIAD OF COMPANIES BUSY DRAWING PLANS AND THEN TRYING TO STICK TO THEM ❞

as technical consultants, suppliers, project managers and programmers. Then you jointly decide on a date that everyone is expected to stick to. In order to achieve your goal, here are some hints that may be useful:

- Try to identify the weak link early on; there is always someone who is overly optimistic but won't be able to deliver on time. Help them to deliver, or replace them.

- Appoint an overall project manager for the whole project plus project managers for each sub-project. Make them personally responsible for the outcome. Ask them specifically if they have taken on the responsibility in question. Make sure you get a yes, preferably in writing. Ask them to explain to you what they have taken responsibility for.

- A culture built on speed is based on the joint setting of time plans and on respecting these time plans no matter what happens. For the CEO, it's about rewarding those who stick to the time plan and building a culture where time plans are real and important.

Now, think about this for a while: as important as it is not to waste time, it is equally important to have a talent for wasting it. To balance structure (keeping to time plans and optimizing time in a project) with chaos (seeing what ideas you get from taking two weeks off to read and surf the web) is an important quality for a business leader. Too much structure might kill the company – and the fun.

The art of doing it right
The first lesson in the new economy is not to try to do everything. There are endless opportunities, and it's very tempting for those running new companies or for those carrying out a change in a traditional company to realize all new ideas that spring up. But in order to create quality, you need to focus. A common mistake is to back too many ideas, too soon. Speed is not about everything – now.

Even though we may be speaking in terms of a new economy, the allocation of scarce resources – the core of economic activity – is key even in newly started companies. Making the most of what you have. Put simply, economizing. The visions are global, the resources minimal. In a start-up or a re-start, there is a constant lack of people, money and time. The business is in reality far too small for achieving all that you want in such a short time. Entering the market quickly can give you a competitive advantage. However, it can also kill off a company that gets lost in the hurry. It is important to understand three central notions:

- quality
- speed
- cost

You always want to achieve highest quality, in the shortest time possible, to the lowest cost possible. The result is unfortunately often the opposite: the quality was terrible, it took a long time, and the budget was overstepped. Who do you blame? Well, most projects get complicated, you know.

What you should strive for is the highest quality, in a realistic time frame (realistic = desired time × 2) to a fair but perhaps high cost. Price should never be the deciding variable in technical projects. If the difference between the highest and lowest price is half a million dollars take the higher price but insist on delivery dates and quality. If you have to place these notions in order of importance, the hierarchy is always 1) quality; 2) speed; and 3) cost. Always work with the best – a prerequisite for success.

To be the first and stay number one
Companies always fight to be first, it is almost a natural law of business. Another law of business is that the pioneers are seldom the long-term winners. Someone launches an idea, but someone else exploits that idea much better in the market.

Apple and Atari pioneered the personal computer, but eventually companies like IBM, Dell, Gateway, Toshiba and Compaq conquered the market. Netscape made the first move in the browser market, showed the way and then Microsoft responded, dominating that market today.

However, Hotmail was first with free, web-based, anonymous e-mail – and they are still number one. Amazon was among the first with a global web-based bookstore – and they are still number one. Ebay was first with a large-scale garage-sale business on the web – and they are still number one. It is precisely *that* you want to accomplish; to be first and stay number one. It is one of the toughest challenges. In the case of Hotmail, they had a six months' lead on the next competitor, RocketMail, and it was enough. Now, they face fierce competition from players like Yahoo! Mail.

How to launch

You are almost never alone with your idea. If there's a market and the time is right, more players will always emerge. It is always very strange to watch; in a market that didn't exist six months earlier you suddenly get three companies launching within a month.

Business ideas are in the air. The question is how to launch them in an optimal way. There are basically two strategies for launching a new idea. The first is communicating your idea well before the launch date, and then keeping on communicating the forward-going plans. This was the typical Boo.com strategy – start marketing the company before it exists to attract attention, talent and capital. The other strategy is about working more in secret, launching when everything is ready, maybe even the customers. Both strategies include the important element of surprise, one of the classic success factors, in business as well as in war. Let's take a closer look at the two strategies.

> **"YOU ARE ALMOST NEVER ALONE WITH YOUR IDEA. IF THERE'S A MARKET AND THE TIME IS RIGHT, MORE PLAYERS WILL ALWAYS EMERGE"**

First attention, then launch

By communicating your idea early on, you can start to build your brand or to claim a part of the future before actually launching. It can scare off potential competitors, but it can just as well attract more companies to the market. They will all say that they had the idea all along. Another catch is that if you have announced that you are going to come to the market with your company or your idea, you have to launch some time. Boo.com, the sports gear retailer, delayed the launch for six months but in the meantime they received a huge amount of press, both good and bad. The trick is to make the market long for your launch, not to talk badly about it. A problem for many entrepreneurs is that there has often been more talk than action; it's much easier to launch a vision than a real product. Avoid this trap.

First launch, then attention

The other strategy is first to develop the concept, test, build, and to launch when the whole thing is ready. Then, you get the attention. There are advantages with keeping a low profile in a new market where there are many competitors, especially if you're not the first one out and can't get all the free media attention that a new idea might attract. Then you have to compete with something else: a superior service or product.

If the product or service is a new concept, i.e. you have to create a new market, it might be good if other companies help you in that task and start creating that market. An example: internet banks were a new concept in the Swedish market in 1996. The first companies to launch got a lot of attention, but it did not give them any competitive advantage in the long run as they actually helped create a recognized mass market for other internet banks (that often had better products). One or two internet banks are an odd phenomenon that consumers might not trust, while eight are an established market that get you acceptance.

What would have been regarded as competition in a traditional sense is nowadays often seen as cooperation as companies actually help each other in getting a new thing accepted.

Let someone else create the market for you, then compete with a superior offering. By working in silence you can also learn a great deal from your competitors as they communicate to the media all the things they are going to do and are doing.

All companies might not want or even have the chance to be first in the market. Usually, small companies have to be one step ahead, while big companies can move more slowly and enter the market later with better resources. The risk with the 'wait and see' strategy is of course that you might not be able to catch up, even with the best resources available. And usually, the large company wins. The typical example, again, is Netscape and Microsoft. Netscape created the market for web browsers in 1994; in 2000 Microsoft dominated it.

The maturity phase is dead
Established companies should practice the discipline of re-starting, that is, view themselves as start-ups. New companies must practice staying start-ups.

When a newly started company has launched, and got its product on the market, it might feel that all is done. The start-up has started, which was the whole point. Nothing could be more wrong and this is probably the most dangerous moment for a new company or project.

You need considerable amounts of personal input, teamwork, and resources to take an idea from vision to reality. But when is the idea implemented? When is it realized? When is it done?

> **❝** YOU NEED CONSIDERABLE AMOUNTS OF PERSONAL INPUT, TEAMWORK, AND RESOURCES TO TAKE AN IDEA FROM VISION TO REALITY **❞**

- Is it done when the idea gets financing?
- Is it done when the idea is launched on the market?
- Is it done when consumers change their behavior?
- Is it done when the idea is generating a profit?

Well, I think it is never really done. Or as Nike likes to say: *There is no finishing line.* It might seem demoralizing that you will never reach your goal, but it's more like a lifestyle or state of mind. It's better to think in terms of milestones, steps along the way. Then you can think:

- Let's celebrate: the idea got financed.
- Champagne for everybody: we have launched.
- It's happening: the market is changing and the idea proves to be right.
- Success: the company is profitable.

But it is not done. When you think it's done, you're dead. It is a trap. Especially when you are a start-up and have started and launched, what do you do next? Well, the answer is simple. When you have started, you just continue to start up and remain a start-up forever. When one thing is launched you simply go on to launch the next. Is that not also true for established companies?

We used to talk about the S-curve. In the S-curve, the start-up phase was the initial stage before the real business started. Just read any handbook on starting a business (except this one). It is usually about the start phase, then the building phase, and finally a maturity phase that will go on for ever into the sunset. It is the classic S-curve. The whole point is to be done so you can sit back, relax and enjoy the success and the profits of an established company.

In the ideas economy there are no S-curves. To start with, there is no maturity stage where you can camp safely after a tiresome climb. The maturity stage simply does not exist, and if it ever did, it is dead now.

Second, if any curve at all is to symbolize a new company or project, it is characterized from the start as an extremely sharp, upwards-turning curve, never fading, but re-starting all the time, or simply dropping vertically when the company disappears from the radar screen as it goes bust or is bought.

The vision for all companies is to be around for ever, and a company is, in theory anyway, immortal. A very old company like the Swedish forest and mining giant Stora (now StoraEnso) has been around for over 750 years. However, I doubt that the majority of new companies will have a life expectancy longer than a few years. It's more about building something based on a great idea, a good team and ambition, then merging with another start-up with an even greater idea or getting acquired by a big company with the resources to take the idea further.

I would call it the V-curve, or rather the A-curve, as it is a 'V' turned upside down. Rapid start, quick death (or transformation into something else). The curve looks like a shark fin or the bow of a sinking boat, whatever you find most appropriate.

The small company can grow on its own, and some do become really large players. But typically small companies quickly get picked up by larger ones, and are transformed into new beings, in a new context, with somebody else's vision of the future.

66 The dynamic nature of the business community leads to the question: what do you really want with your company? Do you want to become rich? Make a better world? Move at high speed and take big risks, or take it easy and be slower, growing in an organic way? Be part of the big boys' merger and acquisitions game? Go public and get the thrills (and anxiety) of the stock market? Or just do your own thing as a private company? You decide. 99

> **❝ IT'S ABOUT DRIVING YOUR OWN, STEEP CURVE UPWARDS, OR CATCHING ANOTHER CURVE MOVING TOWARDS THE SKY AND A PLACE WHERE THERE IS NO FINISHING LINE ❞**

The business community is becoming increasingly dynamic. It's about driving your own, steep curve upwards, or catching another curve moving towards the sky, and a place where there is no finishing line. And so on.

Getting things done (while staying alive)

This chapter has covered small and big companies creating change, but it is the individuals that get things done. So, how do you, as an individual, get things done, while still having a decent life without running the risk of a heart attack? People always have a bad conscience because there is never enough time – for business, for family, for friends, for yourself. Finally, it can break you. This is a personal guide, based on what I have learned for myself and from other entrepreneurs.

Write 'to do' lists

I admit that I live my life by 'to do' lists. But instead of being a slave to my lists, I find it a relief to have the 'to do's in the computer instead of in my head. Whenever I get an idea, have to follow up on a decision at a board meeting, remember that I need to make a call, that I should thank somebody, what movie I should see, what CD to buy, that I need to get flowers, book an appointment, I immediately make a note of it in the 'to do' list in my Palm Pilot. Then, a couple of times every day I go through the list and decide what I have to do now and what can wait. And in the meantime I just forget about it. Sometimes these lists have a couple of hundred entries.

Most of the managers I know make 'to do' lists, and they come in various degrees of sophistication. Some just write down long lists in a Word document, or by hand. I used to write my lists in Excel before getting a Palm. Some categorize them into things like 'business' (with several sub categories), 'health,' 'family,' 'vacation,' (and even 'sleep'!), and so on, with 'private' or 'personal' usually coming last. Taking care of yourself too often comes last, and it should come first.

Make an hour or two every week for a health routine

When I was working like mad building Fondex, I got myself a personal trainer. The point was not really to have a professional to assist me in pumping iron at the gym, but rather to have someone to make an appointment with, with an associated cost if I did not show up. In this way I was forced to go to the gym at least once a week, and after two years it had become a routine (and my body got in much better shape). If going to the gym or taking a jog can be made a routine as natural as logging into your e-mail inbox, then you will survive much longer. I promise.

Put red days in Outlook

A manager for a very fast (and stupid) company who always worked and bragged about never taking time off, once told me that there are no holidays (red days) in Outlook, Microsoft's calendar program. 'We work by Outlook,' he declared.

In Outlook all days look the same. And actually, when I have been working flat out for some periods I have made appointments on national holidays and booked meetings with other people, who also did not realize that the rest of the country was closed. In Outlook's standard version, or in Palm Pilot without the color screen, there are no red days. Christmas is black, Easter is black. (You can actually add color, but most people don't.)

Run your calendar, but don't let yourself be run *by* your calendar. And even if you know that it is a holiday, and you might think this is a good day to work because your phone won't be ringing, take the time off instead and enjoy yourself. It's all right.

Book a meeting with yourself

One of the most efficient ways to get a break is to book a meeting with yourself. During this meeting you can make calls, write notes or reply to e-mails. But it's even better if you use it for something else, to reflect over a decision you have to make, to surf some interesting websites to learn something new, or to ask yourself some really tough questions. It should be a meeting for an inner discussion.

Take time off in micro portions

Apart from booking meetings with myself, I also take time off in micro portions. My three favorite ways to take time off and just relax are 1) taking a long shower in the morning, letting my thoughts stray; 2) taking a long walk, letting my thoughts stray; and 3) taking a cappuccino at an internet café, letting my thoughts stray.

These breaks are really mental breaks that let the brain do something else besides read business plans or e-mails for a while. The brain likes it and, often, because the brain is not under pressure, I get my best ideas and solutions during these micro breaks.

Learn to delete mail without reading it

This is something that I have never managed to do, and I am sincerely impressed by people who can delete mail without reading it. Now, I am not talking about spam e-mail, which I always delete, but real e-mail from real people. I have friends who can walk into the office, check the inbox, find some hundred unanswered emails, delete them all and go to lunch, happy as ever. They reason that 'if it's important they'll reach me anyway.' I don't say that it's always a good thing to delete e-mails mercilessly, but it must be a relief if you can let go of the tyranny of the overloaded inbox.

Personally I think that professional people should reply promptly to e-mails, and take care of their inbox. Management by e-mail is probably one of the most commonly used methods to run projects and a business today. The smart thing to do with e-mails is to have a structured approach to how you handle them, which includes:

- categorizing mail as you get it, by category or priority (can be done automatically)

- taking time off, say, two hours every afternoon, to reply (don't check your inbox all the time, it will make you crazy)

- emptying your inbox every day, if you can, so that you don't have to take care of yesterday's mail too

- learning to delete some mail without reading it, if you dare.

Get another mobile phone

The mobile phone can be a dangerous trap. As it is personal, you normally don't have somebody to filter the calls, like a switchboard. Furthermore, if it is on you can always be reached as you carry it with you. Finally, if it is off, people leave messages that you have to reply to. Once I met an entrepreneur who told me that his mobile phone stopped working after about a hundred messages in the voice-mail. He had to get a second phone to use when the first was full. What a life.

Actually to get one more phone is a good idea, if you never give out the new telephone number except to a close circle of people. Close the first phone, and use the new one. When that phone rings, you know it's either important or from someone you care to talk to. Some people I know got rid of their mobile phones altogether, because they found it too annoying to be reached at all times.

Delegate to others

Delegating to others is probably the best way to get things done and survive. But it only works if you have a great team that you trust, and if there is some slack in the organization. If everybody is stuck with 'to do' lists as long as your own, you can't delegate. What you need is people who:

- have the time and competence for the task

- take responsibility

- deliver the results you agreed.

If you have a great team, miracles will happen. Working with the best is the only way to succeed in business life. You can't do it alone.

CHAPTER THREE

People: The best of the best

I BEGAN TO SEE MY NEED FOR DISCIPLES WHO

WOULD FOLLOW ME EVERY DAY AND WORK AT

TASKS WHERE MY ABILITY WAS SMALL.

NORMAN MAILER, *THE GOSPEL ACCORDING TO THE SON*

To work with the best

One of the best things in life is the opportunity to work with the best. One such person is Richard Normann, a super-intellectual management consultant. We worked together at SMG. Another is Johan Staël von Holstein who is a super-emotional internet visionary. We worked together at Icon Medialab. One has as his motto 'Simplification is the essence of depth,' and the other says 'Kick ass.' (Which motto belongs to whom is your guess.)

Richard Normann started Service Management Group (SMG, later Sifo Management Group) in the early 1980s. He was a pioneer who has managed to get business leaders to understand the meaning of a service economy. For me, he is in many ways a father to the new economy, and he has taught me a lot of what I know today.

There are outstanding people whose ideas one spends a lot of time with without ever meeting the person behind them. For several years I regularly read the articles published in *Wired* magazine, first and foremost by journalist Kevin Kelly who wrote about the new economy (a phrase that must have been born in the magazine some time in the mid-1990s, several years before it became a cliché in magazines and newspapers all over the world). One single article, Kevin's interview with the economist Paul Romer in 1994, probably meant more to me than all the courses I took in economics at Stockholm School of Economics.

❝ Work with the best or don't work at all. This includes employees, consultants, suppliers, and all the other individuals that you and your company are dependent on. As a business leader, you are in the hands of the people you work with. ❞

Your gang

New ventures mean working with new people, regardless of whether you are a Viking planning a plundering trip to Normandy in the 900s or an entrepreneur launching a WAP-portal in 2000. It is like forming a gang. You get together a strong team, give it a name and start fighting other gangs. It is often about recruiting those who can bring something new to the team and who, at the same time, have the competencies needed to run the business.

❝ WITHOUT PEOPLE WHO ARE TRULY BETTER THAN YOU, IT WOULD BE IMPOSSIBLE TO BUILD A PROFESSIONAL BUSINESS ❞

It was Johan Staël von Holstein who taught me always to recruit people who are better than yourself. Knowing your weaknesses is one of the most important strengths you can have. Recruiting those who are better than yourself may sound humble, as if you are capable of nothing. But what it really means is making sure that you are working with people who have real expert knowledge in areas central to the business, where you may not have that much experience. Without people who are truly better than you, it would be impossible to build a professional business.

When I started Fondex, I knew practically nothing about mutual funds or financial systems for fund transactions. At Fondex, I had the privilege of working with some of the best people in the industry. The gang that was formed consisted of professionals within areas such as systems development, fund transactions, finance, law, journalism, and marketing. From the start, they probably didn't know too much about the web, but the gang gradually became what I think was one of the best internet teams in Sweden.

There are few things that give me such a kick as to see people grow and develop and become leaders themselves. If you are about to form your own gang, here's a few tips:

- Give equity and power to key management.

- Respect others' expert knowledge.

- You are building a company together, so don't put yourself in the spotlight at the expense of others.

- Set examples and standards that you can live up to yourself.

- Help others become leaders.

- Recruit high up and recruit above yourself.

- Never let prestige take command – admit your weaknesses, and know your strengths.

- Let everyone make their own mistakes.

- Allow room – loosen the reigns.

Would you like a role in our play?

Recruitment is a crucial activity both for new starters and re-starters. Sometimes I think of recruitment as casting a play. Would you like to audition for a role? There's a script, but we experiment freely around the story. There's the director. Here's the production team. Yes, we have a couple of divas, but that's okay. Our goal? We want to win at least one Oscar. We may have a role for you. Would you like to do a screen test?

Why not see the company as a theatre scene? Spray, the Swedish web agency that was founded in 1995, made their office in Stockholm a marvelous 'stage'. An office with yellow and green walls and bunk-beds where the kids who were employed there slept.

Icon Medialab's huge studio in the trendy area of Värtahamnen on Stockholm harbor was just the same. People came in hordes just to catch a glimpse of the myth. It also looked good in the press. And many turned up applying for a role.

Established companies are rebuilding their scenes to become more attractive. Old-timers such as Ericsson, former state monopolies turned smart telecoms, law firms and big banks, have all donned newer and more youthful suits to attract the right people.

The point is not to put on make-up but to make your company clear, both for customers and for those who may be even more important: the people you want to work with. The American network company Cisco is one of the world's largest companies (measured in market capitalization), and despite already being large they have the ability to carry on growing quickly. One of their key competitive advantages is that they are good at recruiting and keeping people. Smart companies compete for the attention of smart people.

It is said that Cisco once put up a recruitment stand at a gardening exhibition in the San Francisco area. Why? They reason the following. If you go to a gardening exhibition, you probably have a garden to take care of, which means that you probably have a good size house, which probably means that you have a good job with a high salary, and if you live in northern California you are probably making your money in Silicon Valley, which means you are working in the right industry and are therefore an interesting recruitment object for Cisco. If you are a high-tech company and advertise at a gardening exhibition, the chances are quite high that you are the only high-tech company there, which gives you 100 percent attention – compare that to advertising at a high-tech exhibition.

Early in 2000, competition for smart people had toughened further on the Swedish market, not least due to the rapid value growth of internet consultants on the stock exchange – values that were largely based on the number of consultants employed and the companies ability to attract new people. In

Stockholm it was not unusual to find smaller companies trying to recruit people outside the large companies' offices.

Beedo, who ran the community website Dobedo, placed people outside the IT consultancy giant Tieto Enator's head office and handed out fliers with job offers. Mind, an internet consultant, invited passing workers to breakfast in Kista (the 'Silicon Valley' of Stockholm) on their way to work and handed out brochures containing job offers. Those who recruit on the street outside the offices where the people work get more attention than those who squeeze an ad onto the recruitment pages of a newspaper. (Unfortunately, in 2001 most of the people were out on the streets again.)

> 66 To fight in an industry is to fight about the smart people's attention. It follows that you have to get attention in a smart way. Think about how you can build up your own company's scene and how you can make your company clear. Create a Hollywood where new young stars are queuing up for a role in your company. 99

When I recruit

I am going to admit something – I hate CVs. They are boring and often uninteresting. They say nothing about who the person really is. I like to meet people and I use intuition and a couple of easy rules of thumb when I recruit. These are things I find are important:

- frame of reference
- desire to change oneself
- desire to change the world.

Each person has a frame of reference – from education, working life and other personal experiences. Those with a solid frame of reference can quickly adapt to new situations; those with a weaker frame have no map to follow. The frame of reference is often referred to as competence, but I think frame of reference makes more sense. The frame of reference tells me how a person brings the new into their own natural context. This tells me something of their identity.

The next area I look at in a person is the desire to re-evaluate their existing frame of reference and learn something new. Personal development, in a similar way to running a company in a fast-moving world, depends on questioning the old and trying out the new. This means that employees in a company also have to question their own competencies. I see myself as a constant beginner who is starting over time and time again.

Finally, you have to want to change the world if you are to work in a start-up, or a re-start for that matter. Furthermore, I believe that instinct is a good thing in every company. If you don't want to change the world yourself, sooner or later you will be changed by the world. This can be expressed in many ways. It can be called entrepreneurial spirit. At Yahoo! they call it *passion for life.*

It is the overall impression that counts. I think I have a pretty good feeling for people, and the most important thing for me is to find their fundamental theme. We all have a theme. People are complex beings and you can never really know how a new recruit will truly cope with their new job in a new environment with other people. The equation is simply too complicated to be able to make the perfect choice. Therefore I try to find people's fundamental theme instead.

An example. We recruited a person for Fondex to take care of customer administration. She seemed suitable in every way, but what really gave me confidence in her was the fact that she had worked six years in a refugee camp in Southern Sweden. In my mind, I gave her the fundamental theme 'refugee camp administrator.' That was enough for me. I thought that if she had taken care of the world's most vulnerable people for six years, she would surely be able to take care of our customers when they were feeling lonely on the net.

When I have found the theme, I know everything will be okay. I can see that he or she will fit well with the rest of the team. You have to form the gang and build a team that works. If you're not successful with that, you have failed with everything.

Another rule is that, as company leader, you don't have the last say in recruitment. It is the employees that should recruit new people. It is the ones who will be working with this person on a daily basis who should decide whether he or she is right for the job. At Fondex, it was the head of systems who recruited back-office staff and the editor-in-chief who recruited new journalists.

- Decide on key selection criteria for the people you want.
- Formulate questions that will help you understand the person you are meeting.
- Get an overall impression by trying to find the fundamental theme.
- Let the employees recruit new people where possible.

To hire a webmaster – web style

When we needed to recruit a webmaster for Fondex we did not have much time and, as always for newly started companies, not much money. I wanted to find a webmaster who could start before the end of the month. We had used the state-run Employment Agency once before, with good results, and I decided to try it again. And it's free.

The Employment Agency has the undeserved bad reputation of being a social aid to the outcasts of society, in Sweden anyway. This is not so. The Employment Agency is a professional organization with knowledgeable employees and above all, which I like, a really efficient website with a gigantic database accessible to all. The Employment Agency thinks web! That's what I like.

We went into the database and formulated a profile: web programmer with at least two years' experience. The result of this search showed that there were around 300 people in the database that matched. Of those, we picked out all those who had attached a link to their own homepage, following the logic that a webmaster without a homepage is not enough of a nerd to be a webmaster.

A good webmaster must enjoy sitting up half the night testing new programs and multimedia tools and putting them onto a website that flashes and sparkles. That's the type of person you want – someone who experiments and has learnt the hard way.

To those who had their own homepage – over a hundred – we sent an e-mail describing Fondex and asking them if they would be interested in working with us. We received approximately 40 positive replies. To those, we sent out a really qualified profile, a 'job profile from hell' as I call it, with high demands on database programming, C++, SQL, Java, Corba, considerable experience within systems design, software installations and other skills. This profile was highly exaggerated and we were not expecting anyone to respond claiming they had all these proficiencies. I just wanted to see who was up to the challenge. In a fast-growing company, life is full of new challenges, and if you find this difficult, you're not the right person for the job.

No-one lived up to the demands and many backed out. But there were a few, about 10 people, who said that they didn't have all the qualifications specified but that they were willing to learn. To these people we sent further questions and then we asked three to come for an interview. The recruitment process took a couple of days, did not cost anything (apart from time) and the new webmaster started within the end of the month. The person we recruited surpassed all expectations.

Headhunting and selection

There is always the traditional way to recruit new people: hire a recruitment company. There are two types of recruitment companies. One type works with selection and the other with searches.

Selection firms usually place an advertisement describing the company and the job in question. A selection is then made from the replies to the advertisement. The advantage of this method is that the replies come from people actively looking to change jobs, and are therefore probably motivated. You want to recruit motivated people. The disadvantage is naturally that you can't know beforehand who is going to reply.

Companies involved in searches, so-called headhunters, work in another fashion. They build up a database of interesting names in different industries. When they are given an assignment they try to identify suitable people who are later contacted and offered to come for an interview. The advantage with this method is that you are in control of the whole recruitment process. It is quite easy to identify the right people. The problem is that they might not be at all willing to change jobs. Therefore this method is usually more expensive, both in terms of fees to the headhunter and the generous salary one has to offer the candidate.

But there are two general advantages with recruitment companies. One is that they often have access to large networks, have a good knowledge of the market and know which people might be interesting. Selection companies have good networks too. The other advantage is that you save time. Recruitment is time-consuming and small companies often have difficulties in sparing their employees who are fully occupied in the ordinary running of the business. Recruitment companies do the heavy work and single out the best candidates. Most companies also carry out thorough tests, which can be useful as a starting point when recruiting key people for sensitive positions.

“Use recruitment companies if you don't have time to recruit yourself, but remember that recruitment is a key activity and that the right people are crucial for the company's future. It needs to be prioritized. External help with recruitment can be useful for central positions where recruitment must not fail. But if you're talking about a fast-growing business the best thing to do is to free up resources internally for recruitment. Recruitment must be a living part of your company's culture.”

Recruitment at Yahoo!

Today, smaller and smaller groups of people can do much more than was previously possible. Smaller groups of people (i.e. companies) can achieve higher market values. It follows that the people who join the company must be right.

Having said this, it is probably no surprise that Yahoo!, with its around 3000 employees, has given a lot of thought to recruitment. What is interesting about Yahoo! is that they recruit first and foremost a certain type of individual. I understand that they look for four distinct characteristics:

- leadership skills
- people magnets
- zoom-in – zoom-out ability
- passion for life.

When an organization grows quickly the chances are high that those who are working there quickly become leaders. Imagine the following scenario. You have been employed by Yahoo! and start somewhere in the company working with something. Pretty soon a new project is launched and because resources are always a scarcity and everyone else is busy with something else, you get to take care of the project. The project grows and more people start to work there, and after a while the project has become so big that it is time to incorporate it and go international. You are suddenly the boss for a global organization. You may only have been employed there for six months. Academic qualifications are important, but it is more important to be qualified in the company you are working for, i.e. you understand the company's culture and market. You know how it works. This means that a person who has been employed for six months in a company is more qualified than the person who just started, regardless of where they come from. And therefore it is also probable that the person who has been with the company a while automatically moves up quite quickly when new people come in – given that they have the right leadership skills.

Another thing that Yahoo! and many other successful companies look at is the potential employee's ability to attract the right people to the company – how many names of other good people they have in their address book. A person with an interesting personal network can often find a job more easily than someone who is less connected.

Smart companies use their employees to recruit more people and would rather reward employees than recruitment companies. Being a people magnet implies more than just a well-filled address book. It also implies that you are a person who others want to work with. Everyone wants to work with the best. When I have chosen new jobs and companies to work for, it has mainly been because I have found people I could believe in.

Can you zoom in? Can you zoom out? Yahoo! wants people who can focus on one task, maybe for several months to concentrate on getting a result (zooming in). But it is equally important to be able to distance yourself from what you are doing, to reflect and get a broader perspective (zooming out). This is about taking care of yourself, your family and seeing your life as a larger entity where your job is not everything. No company wants people to burn themselves out because they are unable to zoom out from their job and take care of themselves.

Do you have a passion for life? New companies are not about administration, but instead are about building in a terrain without a map. The terrain is explored with curiosity and new ideas. Do you like life? If you have a passion for life you probably have a curious nature. If you have a curious nature, you fit into an entrepreneurial company. More than that: the entrepreneurial company needs you and your colleagues' collective generating of ideas – the future of the company.

Smart people

If you bring together enough smart people you will generate revenues eventually. You could probably create a company whose sole purpose was to bring together a large group of smart people. They would get stock options, high salaries, and everything they wanted. It would be up to them what they wanted to work with.

Venture capitalists, who know what they are talking about, usually say that they don't invest in ideas, but people. What they mean is that if the idea is right but the people are wrong, the idea will never work. If, on the other hand, the people are right but the idea is wrong, smart people will sooner or later change the idea so that it becomes right.

At some point in my life, I would like to start a company by placing an advertisement that looks like this:

Description	Offer	Looking for
– No business concept	– High salary	– People with an outstanding career
– No products	– Partnership	in any business and the will to make a difference
– No services	– Access to capital	
– No brand name		
– No offices		

Then I'd wait and see what happened. I think it would be a successful company. Ultimately, success is about working together. People are the real differentiating factor between success and failure, but the real explanation behind successful companies is smart people who have the ability to work well together. I have seen many companies split up because of intrigues or internal conflicts. I have also seen how smart people tend to be smart because they don't allow personal prestige and retaliation to get in the way of professional conduct and the company's best interests. Smart people make sure it works, if they are smart.

How people will work together is, as I said before, impossible to know beforehand. But smart people tend to be able to balance pronounced individualism with a loyal team mentality. The smart person asserts their competence and pushes their idea, often going against others, but they can just as quickly adapt to the gang. I have seen this happen so many times – smart people arguing loudly about the answer to a problem and the correct way to go. Often all of them are right, for there is no correct answer. It makes me happy to see a group of smart people, each stubbornly fighting for their own intellectual point of view and integrity. You are driving in the fast lane at one extreme where the ego reigns, while all the time you're aware of the other extreme where the gang is more important, and finally the discussion ends with someone being allowed to try out her idea.

"SMART PEOPLE TEND TO BE ABLE TO BALANCE PRONOUNCED INDIVIDUALISM WITH A LOYAL TEAM MENTALITY"

66 Keeping the gang together is smarter that trying to be smarter than the gang. Power games

are not something for young companies. Encouraging each other is the way to go. 99

So what's your job? Find yourself a title!

So, the gang is gathered and it's an impressive group of smart people. But what are they going to write on their business cards? As these new jobs have been created, it has become increasingly difficult to find new titles. During the 1990s it was popular to dream up new and fantastic job descriptions such as 'chief technology evangelist' (instead of head of IT), 'competence coach' (instead of boss), and 'intrapreneur' (instead of project manager). We also came up with webmaster, systems operator, and e-venture manager.

Others removed the title completely because it was seen to be an expression of hierarchy. Personally I think titles create clarity if they tell you what the person actually does. And even better if they can reflect the company culture.

The founders of Yahoo!, David Filo and Jerry Yang, call themselves the company's chief-yahoos. This admittedly signifies some sort of hierarchy with someone at the top. But if the title is chief-yahoo, it hardly feels bureaucratic, but rather a company built on playfulness and passion, which happens to be a central theme in their culture.

In Österlen, high above the green hills near Haväng, on the south coast of Sweden, lies Ravlunda church. It is a beautiful medieval church, quite small, and it looks like most small churches across the country. One simple main building surrounded by a churchyard, which is the last place of rest for the daughters and sons of the parish. The gravestones are simple with simple inscriptions: 'The Fisherman Nils Andersson,' 'The Mason Erik Svensson,' 'The landowner Karl Jonsson,' and 'His Wife Anna.' Is it not beautiful to be able to describe a whole life, not just a profession or an occupation, with one single word? I don't think Wolfgang Amadeus Mozart had any problems with his business card. He probably simply wrote 'Composer.'

Today, more and more people have difficulties in explaining what they do and what it means. There are many new professions that we have not learned to categorize yet. More and more find it hard to answer the question 'So, what do you do?'

Most people make up their own titles. I had a couple of friends who worked for PostNet, a division within the Swedish Post Office that dealt with electronic commerce and business communication. They published a magazine called *eMagazine*. At one point in 1998 they were updating their subscriber database and asked the readers to send in their name, address, industry and title. I got to see part of that material. Over 4,500 people sent in answers and some 1,300 different titles were noted. The experimenting with new titles in the IT industry had begun. There were new professions such as configuration manager, e-mail specialist (but no e-mail postman!), e-manager, help desk (is that a title?), head of internet, and multimedia developer. But there were also many titles from the old economy, such as head of department, union representative and vicar.

There were very few titles that signalled hierarchy. In the 1960s, 1970s and 1980s there were probably more general managers, deputy directors, middlemen and sergeants. In 1990 things started to change. Today, titles denote competence rather than rank. They can even denote personality.

Life magazine did a report on the famous baby-boomers, people born in the 1940s and 1950s. There was an impressive collection of titles given to each and every one of these people who had various occupations and who had gone their own way. Steven Spielberg was called 'The Myth Maker,' Steven Jobs was called 'The Cyber Pioneer,' and Oprah Winfrey was 'The Teletherapist.'

All the smart creativity we are occupying ourselves with today can't easily be explained in one word. It is natural that in a change that tears apart everything we know, we must also fight for our own professional identity and ask ourselves what we, in actual fact, are doing. But remember, to be successful in these chaotic times, you have to be clear, and finding themes, both for yourself and for others, is a good exercise. Sooner or later, what feels confusing will become clear and you can die with your name and a simple description engraved on your tombstone. Is there a more beautiful title than that given by *Life* to Francis Collins, one of those who lead the mapping of the human genetic code: 'Explorer.'

" Today, there is a good chance that you get to choose for yourself what title (if any?) you want on your business card. Whatever you choose, remember that you might have to live up to it. One of my friends, who put 'Vibe Evolver' on his card, eventually evolved so many vibes that he finally separated from the company. "

CHAPTER FOUR

Workplace: The impressionist's studio

I DON'T BUILD A HOUSE WITHOUT PREDICTING

THE END OF THE PRESENT SOCIAL ORDER.

FRANK LLOYD WRIGHT, ARCHITECT

The comeback of the place

What happened to the physical work-place? A trend during the 1990s was to distance ourselves from the office, the place of work, to find new places to work. Preferably at home. If you were a consultant, it usually meant working out of someone else's office. In any case, it was called *distance working*, and it was one of the information society's

> The workplace is your platorm for value creation and your experimental workshop. If you feel that you want to distance yourself from it, you should change jobs, or remodel your place of work.
>
> Have you founded a company, recruited the best people and are raring to go? Think again about the place where you will work together and which philosophy is at the heart of this place. In the long run, the place of work affects people physically, both positively and negatively. And newly started companies need a lot of energy.
>
> Do you have an established company that you are restarting? Manifest the change in a change of office space! Moving offices can create miracles.

experiments. Sure, it's good to be mobile and have the opportunity to work wherever you want, when you want and how you want. But it is not the mobility but the fixed place of work that has meant most to me in my jobs.

It is at the workplace that you socialize with your colleagues – you know, those who are best in the world and who know more than you. It is at the workplace that new ideas and information is accumulated; it is at the office that you have access to knowledge; it is at the office that you have your fixed point.

The impressionist's studio

It was during my time as management consultant at SMG during the mid-1990s that I first came to think of the company as an impressionist's studio. SMG was, on the surface, a strict management consultant firm with, on the surface, strict consultants in strict suits. But that's where the strictness ended at SMG. We were in the business of changing organizations.

This was during a time that the business world, or at least parts of it, had recently started thinking about the future in a new way. Companies stopped looking into their own machines and started asking questions: who are our future customers, what are our future products, what do we want and which direction is the world going in? These were the recession days of the early 1990s. We were in a crisis that was more than just financial and that no one had analyzed. SMG's role was to do this analysis.

It was about exploring the new, challenging official truths, admitting the unknown and learning something about what didn't yet exist. It was about getting people to start thinking, to start discussions about where they were heading in order to be prepared for what had not yet transpired. We used scenarios a lot in our work. We were strategy management consultants but used fairly unconventional methods. Nothing was taken as given and experimenting was the name of the game.

> **❝IT WAS ABOUT GETTING PEOPLE TO START THINKING, TO START DISCUSSIONS ABOUT WHERE THEY WERE HEADING IN ORDER TO BE PREPARED FOR WHAT HAD NOT YET TRANSPIRED❞**

SMG did not have particularly exciting offices. The uniqueness lay in the people that were gathered there and others that were linked through various networks. One example was the Sweden 2001 project, a future study. In order to understand where we were and where we were heading, we invited representatives from different industries from the whole of Sweden: large multinationals, trade unions, politicians, ministries, authors, journalists, professors – over one hundred people flowed in and out of the SMG offices and took part in various workshops. One of the more creative workgroups was busy trying to find new words because we had realized that it was difficult to write about the future using old vocabulary.

Sometimes we moved our experimental workshop out into the wilderness. Bo Ekman, the CEO of SMG, had, during his time as vice-president of Volvo, founded the Tällberg Foundation, a meeting place for new ideas by the Siljan lake in Dalarna, north Sweden. I participated a couple of times. Communication was the theme one time and Bo had invited the top management from AT&T from the US, a couple of people from Ericsson, the internet guru Esther Dyson, the Swedish Minister of Education at the time, Per Unckel, and a couple of other politicians and a number of other more or less well-known faces from the Swedish business community. The former CEO for Telia, Lars Berg was also present. Bo and I went to collect the AT&T group flying in from New York to Dala Airport in their Lear Jet in the middle of the night. (I remember that the airport staff had gone home before we left and left us to close up. Was that allowed? Who knows, everything was so strange anyway.)

The following day, Bo had a show about the development of communication from the Stone Age until now, accompanied by a didgeridoo blaring out of a gigantic, brand new stereo system. In the evening, I gave a theatrical performance with the English Shakespeare interpreter Martin Best. We performed a dialogue from Dougland Copland's *Generation X* during which a real-time chat on the internet was displayed on a wide-screen TV. Twelve fires were lit out on the mountain and the flaring flames were reflected in the computer screen projected on the wall, and the flames mixed with the global communi-cation of global teenagers engaged in a real-time chat. I took a gulp of Coca-Cola, Martin continued reading about modern disillusionment in his best Shakespeare British, and AT&T wondered what they were doing there. That was SMG's impressionistic workshop.

Sometimes we moved into other companies. We spent a considerable amount of time at a telecoms company where we were figuring out how this gigantic company could become more innovative. We soon discovered that it was a company with several different cultures. The telephone division had its own pulse. That was the history of the telephone. The newly started media divi-sion, producing the telephone directories had its own pulse. Market oriented but with a fairly short-term vision. The network division, those who build infrastructure, thought in cycles of 25 years and then there was the ultra-visionary research department.

The first challenge was to get the company's various departments to start communicating with each other. Richard Normann, the founder of SMG, invented the term 'the electric field' which was a symbol for the need to increase the creative conflict in the company by increasing the exchange of ideas between the various departments. And thereby increasing the level of innovation in the company.

❝ RICHARD NORMANN, THE FOUNDER OF SMG, INVENTED THE TERM 'THE ELECTRIC FIELD' WHICH WAS A SYMBOL FOR THE NEED TO INCREASE THE CREATIVE CONFLICT IN THE COMPANY ❞

One of our supporters was a guerrilla fighter from the company's underground movement: the internet. He had founded a portal in 1994, a project that no one seemed to understand. He was constantly frustrated with this large organization that seemed to resist the future. But he liked Richard Normann's expression 'admit the unknown.' Testing is important. He later left the telecoms company to work at a start-up called Framtidsfabriken, now called Framfab and listed on the Swedish stock exchange. The last time I saw him, he had become an internet millionaire and did not seem as frustrated as earlier. And by then his portal was also the biggest in Scandinavia.

Many people passed through SMG's offices in World Trade Center in Stockholm and the other offices in Paris, Helsinki, Copenhagen, and San Francisco. SMG was an impressionist's studio for the future with many crazy and maybe not-so-crazy projects.

"A good physical workplace has a good flow. A flow of ideas and people. It's a place where new ideas want to be born and where people want to be, a place for the unknown and the uplifting. Create such a place.

Create forums for discussion. New ideas are created in conversations about what you are doing. Don't strive for consensus. Conflict is far more creative."

Being in zum-zum

Stepping into the offices of Icon Medialab was probably quite a vivid experience for the majority of visitors who came to the large studio-warehouse in Värtahamnen on Stockholm harbor. That was where the future was being made. This is what you read about in the newspapers.

I started at Icon at the turn of the year 1996–7 when the company was a little more than six months old and had a few dozen employees. My job was to build up the management consulting division, develop new internet projects and work with business development on the web. I liked the company a lot from the start.

Everything was possible. To take an example: I was given responsibility for a new technology to stream video over the internet and we had just written an agreement with the market leader, Real Networks. I had been in San

Francisco at a development conference where the company's founder, Rob Glaser, was speaking and he told us that they would give Microsoft a run for their money (he sold part of the company a year later to Microsoft), and there was also the biggest hero of all, Marc Andreessen from Netscape, who said that video was going to make the internet the mass medium of the 21st century. We have to be a part of this, I thought.

Back in Sweden, in the spring of 1997, Icon launched videobroadcasts over the internet. I invented a channel called Icon Webcast and a program called *Eye to Eye*. The premiere was an exclusive interview with the Swedish Minister of Communications Ines Uusmann. 'Icon starts TV channel' wrote the newspapers and we received yet more press. Starting a TV channel was a total exaggeration, but that was how it was perceived. And everything was possible.

I cannot count all the projects that were born at Icon, the important thing was that Icon's founders had managed to create an atmosphere where ideas and creativity flourished. There was a flow of people, as at SMG, but the architecture was different. Icon was a real studio with a high ceiling where information could flow freely. Sometimes it flowed too freely. The first time I was at Icon in March 1996, music was blaring out of loudspeakers. Half a year later, it was quiet and everyone had headphones instead. You have to have respect for the individual. People's taste in music differs and if you don't respect that, you risk recreating a cigar factory in Havana – an open landscape, yes, but everyone is forced to listen to the same political propaganda on the radio.

The interesting thing about Icon was the company's idea of gathering many different competencies under one roof – programmers, management consultants, behavioral scientists, art directors, media experts, copywriters and so on. That was when I really discovered the strength of the workplace. It was when people who had never worked together previously were gathered together under one roof that an 'electric field,' as Richard Normann would have called it, was created. This 'electric field' made all the difference, and for me it was the ultimate symbol of the ideas economy. That was how I wanted to work from then on and that is how I have continued.

To pass through Icon's offices in Värtahamnen was not like going through any old office, it was like going through a learning trail. You could pass 10 different conversations about 10 different subjects on the way to your desk. You passed screens where things were happening, you passed magazines, books, and everywhere things were happening, there was a constant buzz of information: zum-zum-zum. Everywhere. Being in this zum-zum, with constant dialog going on between different people, creates a creative knowledge, a learning that spawns new projects. Who wants to be distanced from that? (If you want to experience zum-zum in London, book a meeting at financial media company Bloomberg's buzzing office.)

Icon's environment was a model for the sharing of knowledge, practically applied in daily routine. The workplace was a sea of zum-zum where competencies were grouped together, which lead to an intensive sharing of knowledge, especially in the kitchen during lunch. But the company's invisible infrastructure for learning also depended on an intranet where knowledge was gathered and transformed – in the best cases – into structural assets and intellectual property for the company.

66 You have to check the architecture and the mood of the office space where you are working. Is it a place that locks up or frees up knowledge?

If your office is a place where you share knowledge, the reception is a central node. It is by far the most important function in a knowledge company and probably the most trivialized. Promote the receptionist to chief coordinator, responsible for communication within the company.

Let many different competencies work side by side. It's not only a way to generate new ideas, but it also lets people with different backgrounds, educations and jobs get to know each other and develop a respect for each others' expert knowledge. 99

Externally, knowledge was shared with customers via project webs. And every day some employee of Icon was out speaking at a conference somewhere, spreading ideas to the outside world, when the outside world was not visiting the impressionist's studio. A world of zum-zum, hovering around the physical workplace.

When telecom giant Ericsson hired a head of design in 2000 it was clearly a move to raise the level of design of their consumer products, but it could also be seen as a way to increase the tension in the 'electric field.' Ericsson is traditionally a company run by highly competent engineers, but with less understanding for the varying tastes of the unpredictable consumer market. When the share price drops and becomes more and more dependent on the color of the new mobile phone, it's time to increase the 'electric field' in the company and get creative. In spring 2001, Ericsson got desperate and joined forces with Sony to get access to know-how about consumer electronics.

Build hierarchies!

Knowledge companies love to distance themselves from industrial companies, which they deem to be old-fashioned and stiff. Icon Medialab and many other web agencies built up fairly soft organizations, probably because the young founders themselves came from relatively penalizing companies with their roots in industry, an environment where they often didn't feel at home.

When I later built up my own organization, I had made a mental note of the knowledge culture that I experienced at Icon, but I resisted the lack of clarity that existed at the web agencies during the 1990s. Why call organizations 'flat' and those in top management 'competence coaches' when they are really hierarchies with bosses? Hierarchies create clarity.

During the 1990s, a softer approach to working was tested. Young people, and also their employers, started to prefer project-based employment. Being a free agent was popular. From my experience, fixed employment works best, preferably combined with stock options. The reason is that a real commit-ment and passion is needed, full-time, when building a company, and this can never be achieved with project-based staff. It was said that young people worked for desire and that they worked with what interested them. Ideally, we all make choices from the desire and interest to do something. But we also know that once in the company, the day-to-day job involves delivering what you have promised and taking responsibility for what you are responsible for (and in the best cases, taking responsibility for things that do not necessarily fall under your pre-defined area of responsibility).

The truth is that most companies are not driven by desire, but by a sense of duty. This is especially important in a knowledge company where activities are chaotic and where everyone is responsible for creating both order and cre-ative chaos.

A company can start as a hobby, like Yahoo! did, but it can hardly be run as a hobby. During the 1990s, you heard about new companies being run by people who had made businesses out of their hobbies – computer games, for example. But in reality, it is not the hobby competencies but the real, funda-mental competencies that quickly determine whether that knowledge company has a future: fundamental competencies such as languages (to build international networks), mathematics (to attract venture capital), and the spoken and written word (to transmit the idea at conferences).

We spoke a lot about distance working during the 1990s, about the possibility of telecommuting and moving away from the dependency of the workplace. The whole of this chapter is about the strength of the workplace. That is where we create value. That is where we grow. We may distance ourselves from it from time to time, but in order to reflect (or zoom out as they say at Yahoo!) – not because we do not like the place.

I agree with the Israeli airforce when they say that leadership should be done with competence. In Israel, a war zone for many years, experience is often

> **❝ A REAL COMMITMENT AND PASSION IS NEEDED, FULL-TIME, WHEN BUILDING A COMPANY, AND THIS CAN NEVER BE ACHIEVED WITH PROJECT-BASED STAFF ❞**

valued higher than rank. Therefore, it is not unusual for a captain who has carried out a certain type of mission several times to lead a general who is new to that particular mission. This is a hierarchy built on competence, which I think is preferable to a hierarchy built on titles, age and rank.

My philosophy has always been to let the person with the most knowledge in an area lead the project, even if it means that a webmaster delegates work to the CEO. It follows that a company often has two hierarchies: one that has to exist for legal reasons, such as a board of directors and CEO, but also one that arises in the day-to-day operations. Therefore it is naïve to talk of flat organizations, because they don't exist anywhere. The flatness can however be a good metaphor for an open culture in the company where communication flows unrestricted between the various levels and departments in the company. But not even in the flattest of organizations is the whole company allowed to read the board protocols, for example. There are always hierarchies.

Hierarchies can be dynamic and fluid. In the knowledge company where challenges are constantly changing, it is important to accept new, natural hierarchies for every new situation. There is always someone who is best. Let that person lead.

Knowledge companies are perceived to be places where you can develop both yourself and your ideas, and they are. But it is not a cozy sofa. To develop yourself is great, but developing the company and adapting to it come first. Adaptation is an expression of the desire to change; in a knowledge company you have to be prepared to re-evaluate everything you know and be prepared to learn new things. This is often a pre-requisite for functioning in a knowledge company.

❝ THE ABILITY TO PRIORITIZE AND TO ALLOCATE SCARCE RESOURCES IS OFTEN A MORE APPRECIATED CHARACTERISTIC THAN HAVING AN ABUNDANCE OF IDEAS ❞

Ideas are good and the company should be an environment where ideas are born, but it is no secret that your ideas will compete with other people's ideas in the tough competitive environment that exists in a knowledge company. Later on, these ideas continue to compete for scarce resources such as money, staffing

What we thought of work in the 1990s		What it is really about in the 2000s
Project-based employment	vs	Fixed employment
Desire	vs	Duty, taking responsibility
Developing hobbies	vs	Fundamental competencies
Distance	vs	The workplace
Flat organizations	vs	Hierarchies
Developing yourself	vs	Adapting yourself
Ideas	vs	Hard resources

and the time it takes to bring them alive. Therefore, the ability to prioritize and to allocate scarce resources is often a more appreciated characteristic than having an abundance of ideas in knowledge companies, which are usually under severe pressure to deliver on existing ideas.

Project-based employment. Desire. Developing hobbies. Distance. Flat organizations. Developing yourself. Ideas. That was the 1990s. My knowledge company in the 2000s is based on fixed employment with demands of duty and fundamental competencies. The workplace is the main thing, and the culture is built on a hierarchy where you are expected to adapt. This may sound like the 1800s. But I am talking about another type of employment where you are a partner and have a natural participation. Fundamental competencies mean that you have to be able to read, write and communicate in a global world. The physical workplace is a fantastic place, like nothing before it, zumming with knowledge, and the hierarchy is another type of hierarchy which opens up endless opportunities. Adaptation? It is really about the will to change oneself.

Leadership by competence

Knowledge companies are wonderful to work in, but they are not as soft-centred as you might think. A hierarchy based on competence is more ruthless than other hierarchies. In the typical bureaucratic hierarchy with its predictable titles and career ladder, it was easier to hide a lack of knowledge and climb the ladder by rank year after year.

In a knowledge culture, rank is based on competence. Old-timers in the company can quickly be replaced by new recruits with superior knowledge and new ideas.

The system punishes severely and inexorably. This is particularly apparent among programmers who do not need titles on their business cards to tell everyone who is best. Who's best shows directly in the code. The one with the best coding gets the respect and leads the group. Leadership by competence, not by rank. There is nothing wrong with titles. But you have to live up to them.

66 Don't be afraid of hierarchies. Build hierarchies! Don't tear down the pyramids. Hierarchies are good because they create clarity. To pretend that they don't exist is wrong. Accept instead that it is human to create hierarchies. But use them to build a strong culture, not to put people down.

Care for your hierarchy, but don't arrange your office in a hierarchy. Be creative. Put senior management next to customer services so that the CEO can hear what the customers say when they call. Mix the marketing department with the web team so that they can come up with new solutions. Don't let hierarchies draw restrictive lines across your organization. 99

I feel great in open spaces

66 THE RIGHT COMPANY CULTURE IS NOT CREATED THROUGH THE OBJECTS YOU PUT IN THE OFFICE, BUT RATHER BY WHAT YOU REMOVE 99

When Fondex was newly founded and we had just moved into our office space in Hightech center, in the city of Stockholm, the first thing we did was knock down all the interior walls. The right company culture is not created through the objects you put in the office, but rather by what you remove. The office was a big room with an open landscape and a lot of light.

Below the office runs the three-lane wide, heavily congested Sveavägen, like an information highway – a symbol for a flow of traffic on the web, for digital signals and for money. Outside the windows the financial center spread out beneath us.

The open landscape is the perfect environment for a start-up; when everyone is in the same room, communication is much faster.

In the US, large rooms with personal cubicles is the norm: walls surrounding your own little desk form a cube where you sit, not quite isolated from the room as a whole, but still on your own. Putting in cubicles is a cost-efficient and flexible way of using expensive office space, whilst the personal integrity is maintained. But these walls also cut off communication. I prefer a completely open room, without walls between the desks. Like a news room. For a start-up, this is the only environment that works – fast and direct. But it's also a pressure-cooker.

The risk is that those who work in this pressure-cooker are torn to shreds. It is never quiet, it is hard to make personal phone calls, you can always be reached by the others in the room, you are never left alone. The pressure-cooker can explode if there is no culture in the open-plan office. The culture builds on respecting 'personal space' in the big room, and not barging in on someone just because they don't have any walls.

People have a need to distance themselves from others and can become desperate if encroachments on their personal space are too invasive and too frequent. Remember to respect personal space. Here's some advice:

- Instead of shouting across the room, send an e-mail. Usually, over half the e-mails people send are to colleagues who are sitting a couple of metres away. This may seem strange, but it's actually quite obvious. It is often far quicker to send an e-mail than to start a discussion which involves taking time and attention from someone who is occupied with something else. But remember that even responding to e-mails takes time.

- If you have to go over to someone, ask when would be suitable. If it involves several people it is better to meet in a meeting room and send out an agenda beforehand.

- A pressure-cooker is a chaotic environment that requires symbols of order and structure in order for it to work and not boil over. Tidy desks are one such symbol. Having a morning meeting once a week at an exact hour is another symbol, a ritual.

The office is an open landscape – on the surface just a group of people and office furniture. At its worst, it's a pressure-cooker that breaks people down. At its best, it's a balanced combination of chaos and structure that creates fast communication.

One thing that surprised visitors to Fondex was that it was so quiet. Or at least more so than most visitors were expecting from a fast-growing internet company. They had read about us in the newspapers. They had seen us on TV with computers in the background and everyone running around. They had heard about us. And yet it was so quiet. But the computers were humming, people were concentrating. It was a pressure-cooker, I promise, but you couldn't hear it. A revolution is silent when at its best.

66 You have to be sensitive to how the environment is developing and how people are feeling. The constructive can soon become the destructive. 99

Symbols of order
Fondex would have been a very chaotic enterprise, like most other internet companies, if it were not for the fact that the company was a 'regulated financial services company.' Fondex, from the start, had lawyers making sure that the Financial Security Authority's (FSA) rules were followed and that the company acted in accordance with all the laws regulating a financial services company. To be forced to think structure and order is good. A financial services company is only required to keep in good

order the part of the business requiring authorization from the FSA, but I have noticed that it also has positive effects on the rest of the organization as well. Our lawyer used to surf through the whole website at night, going through each and every word to satisfy herself that everything was correct, which led to a culture where everyone made a sport out of creating texts that the lawyer could find no fault with.

At Fondex, there were different symbols for order and morale. One was the portrait of my great-grandfather, the judge Per Arnander. From the oil painting (practically the only thing in the office not from IKEA) in the conference room, he looked down, strict and critical. He knew nothing of the internet and he wouldn't even have been able to imagine what was happening now and probably wouldn't have cared that much anyway. But he would have liked the orderliness.

Another symbol of order and structure was the obligatory Monday meeting. The morning meeting was a way to maintain a routine. The morning meeting is holy because companies need something to be holy. This is at least something that doesn't need to be re-evaluated and questioned every day. In a chaotic environment you should not be afraid of keeping a few symbols of order.

> 66 Think about which routines your organization revolves around and if you need to make more or less of them. It is often better to have a few, important, symbols for order. 99

Excuse the mess, we're refurbishing (again) An organization
and an environment can be right in a specific situation in one phase of the company's life cycle for a certain type of employee of a certain age. In the start-up phase, a large room with free-flowing information can be the right choice.

What happens when we have other demands? What happens when the company enters a new phase? Or when people get older? This question surfaced at a meeting with Svante Weyler, publishing head at one of the leading Swedish publishers, Norstedts. They were in the middle of creating an open landscape in the established company, which was a controversial decision. Putting up walls in a new company can be the wrong thing to do, and it can be equally wrong to tear down walls in an established company. It depends on who is working there and what the culture is like.

For the first time I realized the importance of physically refurbishing the company, often because the office needs to be adapted to the current phase and the current atmosphere.

When I read Po Bronson's book *The Nudist on the Late Shift* with stories from Silicon Valley, I took particularly to a story about an interior design company in Sunnyvale outside San Francisco.

The interior design company, started in the mid-1990s in the internet boom, had specialized in pre-IPO design. What was all this about? IPO (Initial Public Offering) is of course a listing on the stock exchange and pre-IPO is then the time before the listing. At this stage, there is a lack of funds and the company is living on venture capital from benevolent investors. But you still have to have an office that has to be furnished and the balance here is very subtle. On the one hand, you don't want to look like you are spending all the venture capitalists' money on the furniture, but on the other hand, the office has to be cool enough to attract new, hip people. You have to be hip but low-cost. An old factory is fine, but your offices mustn't look like a scrapyard; second-hand furniture is fine, but you mustn't end up looking like a junk shop. And it mustn't cost too much! A delicate job for interior designers. There are also companies specializing in second-hand furniture that have a very fast turn-around. Why buy new furniture? We will be moving/refurbishing/selling the company soon anyway!

In Sweden, pre-IPO design is spelled in four letters: IKEA. That the Swedish furniture giant had become one of the top suppliers to the new economy is perhaps not that well known. But if you visit start-ups in and around Stockholm, you are met by the same tables, chairs and shelves. You can tell the age of the company by the furniture they have: 'A desk from the '97 catalogue? You've been around for a while, haven't you?' The IKEA furniture becomes the company's annual growth rings.

But IKEA is also one of the bottle-necks of the new economy; orders usually take a month to arrive. Hardware suppliers and network suppliers, used to customers who are used to not having to wait longer than an afternoon, tend to deliver the computers and the Ethernet long before IKEA has shipped its flat packages. Visit a newly started company. It is not unusual to see the CEO sitting in front of his new computer, linked to his new network, but sitting on the computer's packaging, waiting for his IKEA desk and chair.

In early February 2000, Fondex moved to newer, bigger offices. They looked completely different to the first ones. This was a result of the company moving into a new phase and becoming more mature. The new offices were still open, but more divided according to the various activities; back office, customer service, editorial, and so on. We had grown out of the explosive pressure-cooker that was needed to kick-start the company and were now in need of a calmer environment, adapted to a daily, more routine-run business.

66 Don't be afraid of moving offices or refurbishing often. It is a hassle moving or rebuilding, but at the same time it's right to adapt the place of work to a business in constant change.

Office space is a bottle-neck in the new economy. Rent enough space from the start. You grow into and out of the space soon enough. And try to negotiate flexible leases! 99

The marble sculpture in the old skunky works

At SMG we worked with a company in San Francisco called GBN, Global Business Network. It had been founded by Peter Schwartz, who was once at Shell, developing scenario methods to help the petroleum giant think the unthinkable and get them to see what no one else was seeing, like the incredible oil crisis at the beginning of the 1970s. The colossus started to think, instead of just drilling and pumping. Then came the next crisis when consumers started thinking instead of filling up their cars, and the environmental movement was born.

One method, as the Californian avant-garde GBN suggested, was 'to put a sculpture in the old skunky works.' The image they had before them was a sooty, oily, noisy, dark factory. People alongside big machines. Hollow-eyed workers resolutely and mechanically carrying out a monotonous job. The emblem of the industrial and mass-producing economy of the 1900s when no-one was expected to think, but just do. What if you wanted to change the company? How do you go about it? Try placing a white, antique marble statue right in the middle of the factory floor. And wait for the reaction. What is it doing there? What does it mean? What shall we do with it? These questions lay the foundations for the change in the whole company. People start thinking. The company starts thinking.

I have tried to fill my own skunky works (admittedly a light office) with objects that trigger reactions. A workplace should be a place where questions are asked, where there is curiosity and where you do not have all the answers. The totally out-of-place oil painting of my great grandfather with a fat stomach and a cigar in his hand was one such object. Who was he? We used to invent answers for our own amusement. Sometimes he was the founder of Fondex, other times he was J.P. Morgan.

Other such objects were eight framed quotations that I put up along the wall in the meeting room. The quotations that are also quoted in this book, here and there, had been taken from people and texts that have caused me to think. Among them are Marshall McLuhan, Richard Normann, Kevin Kelly,

> **"A WORKPLACE SHOULD BE A PLACE WHERE QUESTIONS ARE ASKED, WHERE THERE IS CURIOSITY AND WHERE YOU DO NOT HAVE ALL THE ANSWERS"**

Frank Lloyd Wright and Bob Metcalfe, who founded 3Com. The quotations were not that easy to understand at first glance. They required a certain amount of reflection. All visitors to Fondex passed this wall, but only a few stopped to read them, and even fewer asked what the quotations meant. With the latter, I knew the meeting would be an interesting one. The workplace worked.

CHAPTER FIVE

Culture: The beat in the nightclub

THAT'S THE SPIRIT THAT BROUGHT US FAME!

WE'RE BIG, BUT BIGGER WE WILL BE

WE CAN'T FAIL FOR ALL CAN SEE

THAT TO SERVE HUMANITY HAS BEEN OUR AIM

OUR PRODUCTS ARE NOW KNOWN IN EVERY ZONE

OUR REPUTATION SPARKLES LIKE A GEM

WE'VE FOUGHT OUR WAY THROUGH

AND NEW FIELDS WE'RE SURE TO CONQUER TOO

FOREVER ONWARD IBM!

THE IBM SONG

Finding the groove

You have your company, your nightclub, but it isn't rocking. Maybe you're lacking a basic rhythm, a strong culture in the company. It's the culture that differentiates your company from the others. The culture is the beat in the company around which everything is mixed. A strong culture is the company's guide and leads the company through good times and bad.

Culture is not something that appears out of nowhere; it is created by management. Many think it takes years to build a culture that is later documented in glossy anniversary brochures and oil paintings. Not the case. A culture can be created in a couple of months.

However, a strong and living culture can take decades to achieve. The trick is to decide on what you think is important and then repeat this. But it is also about caring for and cultivating the myth around the company. All companies have a history, even if it is embarrassingly short in the case of many start-ups.

A long history doesn't necessarily mean a strong culture, but in companies where culture has been highly valued, it has been shown that the culture has created a competitive edge. Such companies are IBM, McKinsey, Morgan Stanley, Procter & Gamble, and Volvo. The fact that Ford, another company with a strong culture and history, bought Volvo did not change the feeling of self-esteem in the 'Swedish' car company. The image of quality,

❝ MANY THINK IT TAKES YEARS OF BUSINESS EXPERIENCE TO BUILD A CULTURE THAT IS LATER DOCUMENTED IN GLOSSY ANNIVERSARY BROCHURES AND OIL PAINTINGS. NOT THE CASE. A CULTURE CAN BE CREATED IN A COUPLE OF MONTHS **❞**

safety and robust cars for a modern household still makes Volvo feel closer to Gothenburg than Detroit to many of its customers.

Companies with a strong culture and strong values are usually also able to change themselves, because they have a strong self-confidence. In the same way, a lack of culture, or a culture that is strong in the wrong way, can counteract change. Start-ups get themselves a culture that is naturally based on change and speed, while the culture in established companies can be what prevents them from re-starting. Be aware of the culture and how it steers the company.

I met Amazon's Jeff Bezos briefly in Stockholm in the autumn of 2000. It was a very interesting experience. He did a presentation with no slides, numbers, graphs, or written text. It was just him and a message: 'We are going to create the world's greatest customer experience.' And you believed him, because this was probably the most enthusiastic guy you had ever seen or met; if the whole company culture was influenced by him, Amazon was probably going to make it. He had created a groove in his nightclub.

The vision

Building a culture starts with a vision. There exists a great deal of uncertainty around what a vision really is. For me, a vision is a picture of an idea, and the simpler it is and the more people who can see it, the better.

Microsoft's original vision was 'A PC on every desk.' Ruben Rausing, the founder of Tetra Pak, said 'A package should save more than it costs.' John F. Kennedy said 'Put a man on the moon.'

Often, the simpler the vision, the harder it is to bring about. The vision for Fondex needed several million dollars, many hours and a lot effort (legal changes would have helped too) to bring about the simple and obvious. And one year after the launch the company had still not reached the vision. 'Put a man on the moon' is a simple vision, but an enormously complex task.

There is a hierarchy in business planning and how you think about your company's future. The terms are often mixed up. The hierarchy looks like this:

- vision
- goals
- strategy
- tactic

From vision to culture

Imagine you have set up a web agency. If the company plans to have 20 offices in 16 countries, in six continents with 1,000 employees by the end of 2000, this is not a vision, but a goal. If you say that the web agency will quickly establish itself in new markets where the competition is underdeveloped (in order to achieve cost efficiencies in investment), this is a strategy, and the tactic to get there might be to hire local staff with strong personal networks. On the other hand, I think the idea of a 'global web agency' is a vision.

For Fondex, the *vision* was to build a marketplace for all mutual funds at one address. One *goal* was to have a large number of customers and a certain accumulated wealth in the customer accounts at a certain point in time. The *strategy* for this was to start the marketplace and sell all the funds before we had written contracts with the fund companies, and offer good services to our customers saving in funds. By being of use to the consumers, we would begin generating volume, both in traffic and money, and with this volume as a base, we would later on sign agreements with the fund companies to receive commissions from them, which would be our primary source of income.

Part of the *tactic* was to establish a professional relationship with the fund companies, attract partners to build up the customer base, to constantly develop new services for the consumers, and to create new usefulness on the internet. See! By breaking down the vision into goals, strategy and tactics, natural priorities arise – as do values. One of the strongest values in Fondex was to focus on user needs – the website must be easy and effective with good, unbiased content to attract new customers. A strong part of the culture at Fondex was to always think from the customer perspective, to see Fondex and the website not from your own perspective, but from the eyes of the customer. This is something that the management repeated every day: 'Think from the customer perspective! 'Think web! Look from outside and in!'

When an organization grows and more people come into the company, the company changes. This is natural. But in actual fact, it is not primarily more people coming in but new ideas about how things should be done that causes change. The company often develops in a way that you had not expected, with respect to details. The main thing is that the majority of people are with you on the vision.

To be honest, Fondex supermarket-vision was actually realized, but it was harder than expected to reach the goals and the grand plan failed when the market dropped. However, the vision and the strategy created focus and a very strong culture.

❝ How would you formulate your company's vision? There might already be a statement, but it is likely that it reads as a goal or a strategy instead of a real vision. Does the vision have genuine roots in the culture? Does the culture have genuine roots in the vision? ❞

Values

A strong culture is expressed by strong values. Sometimes they are written down so that everyone can understand what is important in the company – employees, customers, investors and everyone else that may be interested. It creates clarity.

You have to work with the best. You also have to have the best competitors in order for your own company to develop. The internet trader E-Trade established itself in Stockholm at about the same time as Fondex. They are among the largest in the world in trading stocks over the internet and they are good at what they do.

E-Trade takes pride in its values and the company writes them down clearly in its annual report and on its website so that no one can miss what they stand for. First of all, they tell you their vision. For example, in the 1998 annual report the message was 'The future of investing.' Then they tell you about their strategy: to build revenues by building brand awareness, creating new content for customers with new demands, to reinvent the industry through new technology and finally, to develop the opportunities in a global world and to expand its services to new markets. Already in the vision and the strategy lie the foundations for the values in the company.

But nothing is left to chance, and so that no one has to wonder about the values at E-Trade, they are also written down. CARE: Customer-focus, Agility, Reliability, and E-innovation. This could be any company and values do have a tendency to become general. This doesn't matter. The main thing is that they keep the company together and are alive in the organization. And they create focus.

The theme of the vision might change from time to time. But not the vision. In E-Trade's 1999 annual report, the slogan was 'Championing the power of the individual of the 21st century.' It's still about the future of investing but the core values of the company have been honed down even more to focus on the individual, and the world of possibilities that the company offers its customers. It encourages the individual to take advantage of the newly won freedom. Yes, E-Trade is on a mission and if you read the annual report you could almost mistake it for a political program; they talk about human rights, civil rights, democratizing individual personal services, breaking barriers, and of course the revolution. But, it's about brand-building, and culture-

❝THINKING ABOUT CUSTOMERS, BUILDING TRUST AND CUSTOMER SATISFACTION QUICKLY BECOMES A NATURAL PART OF THE CULTURE IN AN INTERNET COMPANY❞

building. Thinking about customers, building trust and customer satisfaction quickly becomes a natural part of the culture in an internet company, where the customer's presence is noticeable, direct and perpetual in a business that is open 24 hours a day. Seven days a week. All year round.

" Can you write down the most important values in your company? Are they written down somewhere? Are they alive in the company? **"**

" Do you know what your own personal values are? Are you able to write down five words that describe your own personal 'culture'? **"**

Heroes, Growth Engines and Guides
It is the Heroes in the company that symbolize the culture. I suppose I was a 'Hero' in Fondex when we launched, since, as the company's founder I symbolized the vision. As a hero, you have a responsibility to keep the vision alive, and do it every day.

When Fondex was launched in May 1999 the company received a lot of media attention since it represented a new phenomenon in a large market. During the following months, Fondex was mentioned in several hundreds of articles in the Swedish and international press. The board had decided that I should give the company a face and this was only natural. A lot of the press was therefore about me, with pictures of me and quotations of mine. After a while it seemed that the company was made up of only one person.

Leadership is very much about creating new Heroes. In August 1999 our newly recruited CEO started. Qualities needed to start up a business are different to those needed to keep the business going, and my role was to continue building new companies, whilst the new CEO's role was to run the Swedish operation. My role was also to introduce her as the head of the Swedish operations and make her a symbol of Fondex. She became a new Hero at Fondex.

Growth is brought about by ideas that become companies. But in order for the ideas to gain momentum, a collective of people are needed.

Within companies there are always qualified and driven key people, and the company's development depends to a large extent on these high-achieving individuals – I would like to call them Growth Engines. The company grows around them, and thanks to them. Companies should focus on these Growth Engines and create an organization that supports them. Growth is achieved by people. Lubricate the Growth Engines! They are what make the company grow.

The Growth Engines are also Guides in the company and serve as good examples to others. A culture is successful if the rest of the company strives to be as good as the Heroes, and is unsuccessful if the best lower themselves to the lowest common denominator.

“ As founder of a company, you have to give responsibility to people and help them develop into heroes. The hardest part is stepping aside and not interfering. Creating new Heroes is more about bringing people out, rather than steering them. ”

You have to bring out people who have taken initiative, overcome challenges, and been successful. This is especially important for new recruits. As a new employee, you always feel small and lost. At such a time, becoming a Hero is a great feeling. (Both Terrance Deal, professor at Harvard and Allan Kennedy, from McKinsey, have written insightfully about heroes in business.)

You-Think culture

What characterizes successful knowledge companies? They have collective insight, and act on it. The collective intelligence in a company is always greater than the limited knowledge of each individual or a management team that cannot or should not make decisions on a myriad of questions. This is why it is important to delegate decision-making power and responsibility in the organization.

Successful companies are flexible and world leaders at constant change. This is partly achieved by letting the organization make the daily decisions that make up the company's total development, guided by the overall vision and goals.

Strong cultures are built on responsibility. I call it a You-Think culture, a culture where people can, do, and are encouraged to think for themselves. And act.

For me, this means encouraging people to take on responsibility for themselves, rather than giving it out. Knowledge companies must be active. I measure leaders by their ability to take responsibility, in the same way that I regard my most important quality as leader to be encouraging others to leadership. As a leader, you are dependent on others, and to manage is therefore about being able to delegate to others. And I don't like interfering either. My goal is simply to be superfluous, to not be needed.

> ❝ MY GOAL IS SIMPLY TO BE SUPERFLUOUS, TO NOT BE NEEDED ❞

Taking responsibility is an active thing because it necessitates the identification of a task, suggesting a solution and delivering a result. In other words, it necessitates thinking for yourself. A knowledge company is not just a group of incredibly qualified and competent people, but a group of people who can think for themselves, and act on it. The opposite of a You-Think culture is a Punishment culture where someone hands out orders, makes sure they are carried out and hands out sanctions if they are not.

Both the You-Think culture and the Punishment culture probably work quite well. A research laboratory at healthcare giant AstraZeneca and a unit of the Foreign Legion in North Africa are probably both effective organizations.

The worst type of culture, one which has to be avoided at all costs, is an Oops! Culture. 'Oops! was that my responsibility?' 'Oops! how time flies, were we supposed to deliver by November 1?' 'Oops! should it have been an SQL 7.5 server?'

Each time I hear the expression Oops! in an organization I feel ready to cry. It is a sign that no one has thought for themselves or that no one has received orders from someone who has been thinking. It is a no-man's land where no ideas exist. Fight Oops!

> "People need knowledge and authority in order to take on responsibility. Taking on responsibility also takes courage. Give people the courage to become leaders and then make sure they have the knowledge and tools they need to take responsibility."

> "Develop people who are working hard at fulfilling their responsibilities. Do this by showing respect for their competence. Express this respect concretely in the form of a pay rise, stock options and room for maneuver."

> "Build up the employees' belief in the vision by showing the company's belief in its employees."

Take responsibility for you, nobody else will

People can get burnt out as fast as a hard disk can crash. It happens sooner or later, especially in an extremely fast-growing company, where you go from a PowerPoint presentation to launch in a couple of months and continue to launch new versions without a break. Taking responsibility is also about taking responsibility for yourself. I often get asked who is responsible for the well-being of the employees. The employees themselves, is my answer.

❝COMPANIES SHOULD BUILD A CULTURE THAT ENCOURAGES ITS PEOPLE TO TAKE CARE OF THEMSELVES, BUT THE ACTION, THE DECISION TO GO TO THE GYM OR TO TAKE A WEEK OFF, IS UP TO THE INDIVIDUAL ❞

Companies should build a culture that encourages its people to take care of themselves, but the action, the decision to go to the gym or to take a week off, is up to the individual. The most important thing is the attitude of the senior management at the company. Every time someone asks me if they can take some time off, I say of course, that's up to you. I want everyone to feel that it is all right to take some time off, and I do not ask why. If the reason is that someone is tired and needs to rest, all the better. In my opinion, this is the most valid reason for time off, and when I take time off, I tell it like it is 'I need to rest.'

❝I need to rest for a while! Teach yourself to say this and teach others to respect it. Teach others to say it and respect it. I need to rest for a while. However, a person who needs to rest often is probably not the right person for a fast-growing enterprise.❞

At Fondex, we were about to recruit someone who would be responsible for establishing Fondex in the Nordic region. He had a long and impressive CV and I was ready to sign an employment contract. But just as we were about to sign on the dotted line, he wanted another clause added to the contract: the right to two months' annual leave. I immediately became suspicious and when the rest of the company heard about it, everyone reacted very strongly

– he can't work here, he doesn't understand our culture. I was forced to rethink. On the one hand I didn't necessarily have anything against someone taking two months off if they needed to do so in order to do a good job, but on the other hand, it felt wrong to have to write it into the contract. The fundamental rule is first to be willing to work hard, then you take off as much time as you need to. This person wanted to do the opposite: first have the right to a lot of time off, and then be willing to work as much as was needed of him. It was not about adding a clause to the contract, it was about adding a new culture to the company.

In companies with strong cultures, the sense of responsibility is often strong. This means that the employees tend to put their work before their own free time and their health. Duty must never come before health. People's health always goes before the company. Helping each other to take care of one another is a good thing; encourage others to take some time off if they need it. Taking care of one another is everyone's responsibility. For example, the founders of Icon Medialab labeled the company a 'feel good company.'

Our agenda

Plans change all the time; you have to compromise and think things through all over again. It is natural. But there is a difference between scrapping a project because it is strategically wrong and scrapping a project because you didn't have time or because you started too late. Oops! You should always count on the challenge being bigger than you thought at first. Complexity and difficulties must never come as surprises in a start-up, where the unexpected and difficult planning are part of everyday life.

Danger is around the corner when the culture slowly begins to slide from 'How shall we achieve these goals?' to 'How shall we lower our goals in order to achieve them?' When I saw this happening in my own organization I felt like a loser. 'Oops! I never thought it would be this difficult. Had I known, we would never have set these goals.' To hear that made me mad.

Build a culture where you, as a company, set the agenda: our agenda. We decide, then we take action. This means that you do what is needed in order to get where you want to be. Build a culture where you ask yourself 'What shall we do in order to achieve our vision?' without having to ask someone else for permission or lowering the goals.

Every day, the management team needs to fight for its own goals and its own vision which steers the enterprise. Our agenda.

To build an aesthetic culture
Try to build an aesthetic culture. The web interface is a symbol of security and trust in the same way that a bank in a stone building with a marble entrance signifies that your money is safe in a vault somewhere when in actual fact it consists of a series of ones and zeros on a magnetic strip somewhere in the system. A web company builds trust by managing everything that leaves the company, via the web and e-mail, through its aesthetic interface to the outside world. Here are three examples of what happens when a culture is not aesthetic:

" A WEB COMPANY BUILDS TRUST BY MANAGING EVERYTHING THAT LEAVES THE COMPANY, VIA THE WEB AND E-MAIL, THROUGH ITS AESTHETIC INTERFACE TO THE OUTSIDE WORLD "

- **Week 42**. The same newsletter goes out three times. There is something wrong with the database we use for mailing. For the subscribers, who are usually swamped with e-mails, it is annoying to get superfluous mail. Some subscribers cancel their subscriptions.

- **October 5**. We conduct user tests with a market research company. Two focus groups are testing the website. In the discussion afterwards, one lady commented, 'I found spelling mistakes on several pages and this does not inspire confidence. I would not feel safe putting my money into an internet company who cannot even spell.' One spelling mistake on a website is just as bad as a broken window at the bank.

- **October 22**. We send out two press releases to the media. The problem is that they do not have the same typeface or layout. I had written one of the press releases and someone else had written the other. Oops! All the journalists who received these texts must have thought that we were running a shabby operation.

It is not particularly expensive to be aesthetic, but it is costly to be non-aesthetic. The aesthetic aspect is becoming more and more important for companies. Business leaders must think web style and realize that the web is the company and the web is the product, since many customers will have their relationship with the company via the web. The quality of the company is determined in a second.

In the future, organizations will become more aesthetic. The future is more aesthetic. Aesthetic values take on greater importance. Consumers, for example, are becoming very adept at deciding whether they have come to a good interface. This decision is made in a couple of seconds. That is why the interface is so much more important than marketing. You can get a customer to the website by marketing, but then aesthetics takes over. If the first impression doesn't mirror what the marketing has promised, the whole marketing effort is wasted. Few people come back after a first bad impression.

To build a knowledge culture

During the first half of the 1990s, the 'production culture' was reinforced in the industrial world. The dominating theme in western companies was rationalization and increasing production efficiencies. Increasing global competition, driven by deregulation, recession, growing economies in Asia, and increasing globalization of capital, was taking its toll. The answer from management teams was to streamline organizations, sell off operations that were not core to the business, cut costs, reduce headcount and increase productivity, i.e. increase output per unit of input.

Concepts such as Business Process Reengineering (BPR) and down-sizing spread across the world. Thousands of jobs disappeared over a couple of years from within the Swedish banking industry alone, due to rationalization, closed branches and internet banking. The industrial giant ABB launched its T50 program which was about reducing lead times in production by 50 percent. This was successful and productivity rose. If you want to be competitive, you have to make use of your resources as efficiently as you can.

For most companies who underwent some form of rationalization during the 1990s, the rationalization was most likely necessary. But it was also a sign that the economy was governed by a production culture. When the competition increased, many chose to optimize their production. In a production culture, saving time is important, as in ABB's T50 project.

More and more companies discovered, however, that they could not continue to be competitive simply by saving and streamlining. You have to develop new products, look for visions of the future, look out towards your markets, and ask yourself how it is changing out there and then create new offers for a new world. It is about generating new knowledge, not just once, but every day over and over again in order to stay competitive.

Funnily enough, big corporations have embraced the new thing – the internet – as a way to further reduce cost and increase efficiency in its 'production culture,' handling both customers and supplies on the web. This is good.

THE ABILITY TO GENERATE IDEAS AND TO BE ABLE TO SYSTEMIZE THEM IS WHAT DIFFERENTIATES THE CULTURE IN SUCCESSFUL KNOWLEDGE COMPANIES

The knowledge society is not a place where you stuff in more education (as many believe), but a place where an unpredictable chaos reigns and where knowledge is generated constantly. A knowledge company is a place where ideas come to life.

The ability to generate ideas and to be able to systemize them and turn them into structural capital and competitive edge is what differentiates the culture in successful knowledge companies.

Be aware – knowledge costs

You could say that all companies are knowledge companies. If you are running a business, you need specific competencies. But there are companies who, in a purer way, build their business on the production of ideas. This is the case for a consultancy, for example, which is confronted daily by new customer problems that they have to solve with creative ideas. This is also the case for many established companies in constantly changing markets requiring new solutions and new ideas all the time.

Production is fairly expensive when you use knowledge as the raw material. Individuals with high competencies cost, since the market value of the raw material knowledge is high. Knowledge companies mean high salaries, bonuses and generous stock-option program where founders and shareholders have to share their stock with the employees.

Equipment is a big financial cost and knowledge workers want the latest computers and fastest internet connections. At a start-up company, there is always a pile of empty cardboard boxes from newly bought hard drives, WAP telephones, iMac screens, digital cameras and Palm Pilots. However, this is marginal compared to what it costs to buy consulting hours from Prada-clad self-assured programmers and project managers with high hourly rates.

OK, so it's cheap to send an e-mail. Digital communication is probably the part that costs the least, even if the telephone bills in a knowledge company are sky high due to all the surfing and constant broadband connection to the internet. But all the contact via the net leads to the need to meet face to face from time to time, like traveling to Silicon Valley. Building networks is just as much about building a knowledge network by traveling and meeting up as it is about technology.

Companies in industries such as raw-material intensive industries or forestry are, of course, also capital intensive. An investment in a new rolling mill in a larger thin sheet steel factory, such as the one made by Swedish Steel in

Borlänge, cost some $200 million. But the price per kilo for steel is roughly the same as the price for potatoes – under a dollar.

The price reflects a low raw material price. The complex production process demands maximum productivity and the shortest lead times possible to keep the price down on an international market with fierce competition. Naturally, there is also a knowledge content in the steel – to produce thin sheet steel that is light but strong – for which you can charge a little extra.

In comparison, the end product in a consulting firm in the new economy costs $100–300 per hour in consulting fees. This price reflects the high price of the raw material, knowledge.

The production economy and the knowledge economy are in many ways each other's mirror image. But it is wrong to think that it might be cheaper to run a knowledge company just because it isn't a steel mill.

❝ Be prepared to pay to build your knowledge culture. Raw materials and production require big capital investments. Knowledge costs, but it is also right that you have to pay to gain access to the highest competencies. **❞**

From material to immaterial transfers

When smart people work together they become even smarter. When less educated people work with highly educated people, the 'dumb' ones learn from the smart ones.

❝ WHEN SMART PEOPLE WORK TOGETHER THEY BECOME EVEN SMARTER **❞**

Welfare, in the old industrial era, was built largely upon material transfers – transferring money from the rich to those who were poor, through taxes. And if someone became rich, in a social democrat country like Sweden, it was often seen as proof of someone else becoming poorer – a zero-sum game.

In the knowledge era, the reverse is true. If someone is rich, the people around that person often become richer themselves, because a series of intellectual transfers occur – knowledge transfers. At a knowledge company, hundreds of intellectual transfers occur every day, since different people with different competencies and different ideas learn from each other. In the long run, it is better to support intellectual transfers than material ones since long-term growth in the economy is based on intellectual capital.

" No one is as smart as everyone together – share ideas with others. Become the one that other smart people want to be with. Encourage the sharing of ideas. "

The sharing of knowledge is not something soft in a knowledge company, it is an economical prerequisite and a part of the culture. Sharing knowledge is a duty. If smart people kept their ideas to themselves, the development of the company would be negatively affected. The transfer of knowledge is everyone's duty. Keeping knowledge to yourself is theft.

" THE TRANSFER OF KNOWLEDGE IS EVERYONE'S DUTY. KEEPING KNOWLEDGE TO YOURSELF IS THEFT "

The transfer of knowledge doesn't only have to occur at work. It is a civic duty for knowledge workers to transfer what they know and to start discussions and build a knowledge culture even outside their own companies. Otherwise they risk becoming victims of the divide in society that they are helping to create.

In early 2000, I started a project called Transfer. The idea was to create an exchange: those working in the high tech industry and other spearhead industries would go out to schools in the suburbs and talk about what we do. Now, in 2001, the project is growing with an increasing number of sponsors and members who want to bridge the digital divide in our society.

The aim is to transfer knowledge to those who may not come into contact with my world and to inspire entrepreneurial spirit. The hip-hop artist Lauryn Hill has said that the difference between people is not ability, but access (her Refugee Project). I agree. Transfer is about increasing the access to knowledge.

But this is not simply born out of charity; we are doing this for our own sake, too. Knowledge workers live an isolated life in their high tech companies and seldom have any time to spare for other parts of society. To go out and learn something new and meet people that you may not otherwise meet is a real high! And in this way we learn something new too, and the transfer of knowledge occurs in both directions.

Intellectual transfers are also needed between those who already have access. In February 2000, I founded a forum called E-commerce Round Table together with Ola Lauritzon, then CEO at the internet company Epo.com. This was a group consisting of CEOs and founders of internet companies. We met once a month (but e-mailed each other regularly) in order to discuss industry questions and to learn from one another. Start-ups are, as I have said, companies where you write your own handbook, and the meaning of E-commerce Round Table was to share some of your handbook with others.

A good friend, the Swedish philosopher Horatius, would probably use the term domain for something other than an internet address. According to him, a domain is a homogeneous interest group with its own frames of reference, for example, musicians, athletes or business leaders. What is interesting is not what happens within the domains – when, for instance one telecom company buys another – but what happens when the boundaries between domains cross over. The knowledge society needs such domain-crossing activities. That is where the new ideas can be found. So let us also go beyond and across our domains.

The elite in the elite companies
The knowledge society has created more elitist groups and elitist cultures (or domains). We have moved from a society with one elite to one with several elites. This is partly due to a society with many possibilities of expression where we are forced to choose an identity, and partly due to an increasing specialism based on expert knowledge. The best example is perhaps the web which is full of elite groups with their own expressions and cultures. In the diversity, there is no room for masses.

Other typical elite groups are graffiti artists who are charged with damages and become the elite within the graffiti world, hackers who are an elite on the internet and Hell's Angels who are an elite among motorbike organizations. Elite groups have their own measures of prestige beyond the established society.

The elite in the internet society are those who build the technology, lay down the infrastructure and produce the content. Elitism always builds on a unique knowledge, but not always in the normal meaning of the word. Becoming an elite is more about creating your own world and then mastering it.

Being elite is about being the best at what you do. It is also the driving force behind every knowledge company. All knowledge companies therefore have to, by definition, aim to be elite companies in order to be competitive. The knowledge society, with its intellectual differences, creates gaps in a whole new way compared to the industrial society, where material differences could be evened out fairly easily. But we may not want to even out the differences since diversity creates competitive edge.

Within the knowledge company, there are a whole lot of different elites, each with its own characteristics and rituals. Respecting competencies is to respect different elite groups. Examples are the elite 'legal staff,' 'technicians,' and 'journalists.' Each has its own knowledge culture. The legal culture is based on clarity, the technicians' on logic, and the journalists' on integrity.

The programmers are perhaps the most noticeable elite in the internet society. It is not a coincidence that the top representative of the digital elite, Microsoft's founder Bill Gates, left the administrative post as CEO in January 2000 to focus instead on the significantly more elitist post as head of software architecture, the chief priest for the development of code.

"Those who do not understand how elite groups work and think will find it difficult to run a knowledge company. Identify elite groups and get to know their cultures."

About men and women Gender has become a key issue in the high-tech society, maybe due to the lack of women in general. When I speak at conferences, I am often amazed that the panel is comprised solely of men whereas the debate leader is quite often a woman. It is as if high tech conferences have become a way for women to get to the bottom of what the men really are up to. And there are two things that women always ask about: How burnt out people are, and the division between men and women in the companies.

To me, it is natural to have half the workforce made up of women and half of men. This is not due to the political correctness of having an equal proportion of the sexes, but it is founded on the fact that the usual market comprises half women, half men. The division of the workforce is a natural consequence of the division of the users. Consumer companies have to be practical and pragmatic about their attitude to the outside world and they have to work with realities.

For example, a website is often perceived differently by men and women. The first version of Fondex's internet service, which was launched in May

1999, had been through user tests consisting of male and female focus groups. The women perceived the prototype to be boring and square, which led to a change in design before the launch, making the interface more rounded and softer. But the content was still quite 'masculine,' with stock information, trading accounts and diagrams in a conservative blue color. At that time, there was a clear majority of men working at Fondex.

As Fondex grew and more women entered the company, the culture changed slowly. This was reflected in the website. Many of the women at Fondex couldn't identify with the image on the web and the result was a newer and more accessible style of logo, a softer content, other colors, and more information. This was not solely the women's doing, but the need for change came up in the strategic discussions we had in the company about how the website needed to look and be perceived by the users on the net. The discussion was colored by professional opinions as well as male and female perspectives. There is value creation in a culture that is both masculine and feminine.

In fast-growing companies where new decisions have to be taken in a chaotic and insecure environment, the level of conflict is always high. It does not become easier when you add a male and female dimension to it. But knowledge companies must strive to increase friction. The friction that occurs between men and women will probably generate ideas that are superior to those generated by solely male or female cultures.

"IN FAST-GROWING COMPANIES THE LEVEL OF CONFLICT IS ALWAYS HIGH. IT DOES NOT BECOME EASIER WHEN YOU ADD A MALE AND FEMALE DIMENSION TO IT"

My kind of culture
This chapter has been about building culture, what culture is made up of, and what I believe are important values for a company. I guess that if I were to summarize the five main values in my culture, frame them and hang them up on the wall, they would look like this:

one	revolution
two	duty
three	beauty
four	independence
five	curiosity

Some grand words, you think. However, the culture in a company begins with a vision, which is usually about the new customer value. This is the belief that you offer a superior service in a market and that the idea is so big that you can create a revolution – for the customer and end-user of your service or product. The person who is only after a mediocre change will probably not be able to build a successful business. Go for revolution, but be aware that new companies seldom create revolutions as big as Netscape or Napster did.

Duty is about taking responsibility and about the belief that it is the people and their ideas and competencies that drive the company forward. That everyone is expected to use his or her intelligence and professionalism to take responsibility for the development.

Beauty is the belief in the aesthetic surface as a symbol for a company that is well organized beneath the surface as well as on top. For any company in cyber space with a screen as its contact with customers, the aesthetic value becomes crucial to success.

Independence is based on 'our agenda' and the belief that we plan, and we carry out those plans. You must believe in what you do and how you act to realize your ideas, regardless of what challenges you face.

Curiosity is the belief that no one has the complete knowledge for making the right decisions in every new situation and that you have to experiment, and even be allowed to fail, in order to acquire new knowledge. Curiosity is the motor in a knowledge society.

CHAPTER SIX

Interaction: Think web! Think human!

THE VALUE OF A NETWORK GROWS AS THE

SQUARE OF THE NUMBER OF ITS USERS.

BOB METCALFE, FOUNDER OF 3COM

All companies are web companies All companies are essentially
web companies, or will be so, in the sense that they will be communicating
with their customers via digital interfaces such as the computer screen, the
PDA or the mobile phone. And that's when the company becomes what the
customer sees on screen. Can you imagine a serious company without a website today?

For companies starting up on the internet, this is obvious. However, for companies who are used to and like living in the physical world, it is about
rethinking and becoming a re-starter in the network economy. Think web! It's
part of the job.

The website where you should spend most time is without a doubt the one
that belongs to the company where you work. Each day, spend at least some
minutes on it – even though you have been there hundreds of times before –
looking for updates, making sure changes have been made and whether new
services have been launched yet. At Fondex, I was constantly thinking
about how the website could be improved and was constantly worried
about whether it was informative enough, whether the service was up to
scratch, if texts were wrong, whether the registration or the logging-on func-
tions were working properly, or if there were other faults that negatively
affected the user.

There was always something that could be done better, and I always thought in terms of the interface as seen by the customers. I was never totally satisfied. What made me really happy was when I logged on and saw improvements. Someone in the organization had come up with a good idea and had raised the level of the website a couple more notches. That's when I knew that the culture in the company was working.

The web as an extension of the user

What is a customer? For a long time the customer was seen to be a receiver of products. A company, such as the motor company Ford, made the production process cost efficient and optimized every step in the chain, in order to offer standardized products to the customer at an affordable price. Certain companies spent their time vertically integrating. They owned the whole chain, from mine to factory to distribution and, in certain cases, even the customers, as in the old mining society. Producing companies saw as their mission the distribution of their products to the people. The typical value chain looked something like this:

Raw material → producer → wholesaler → retailer → customer

When the consumer began to move around more and the mass became more heterogeneous and complex, companies began to think of the customer as a source of information. You wanted to learn more about the customer in order to develop new products, market them better and sell more products. The challenge for the companies was to create strong relationships with their customers, and in this way the customers also came closer to the companies. Another way of expressing this is that the value chain was turned back to front and the customers' needs came first so that you could understand what you needed to sell to these customers.

Needs → product development → marketing → customer relations

The third step, one could say, was to see the customer as a co-producer. We not only create relationships and research customers, we also invite them in to participate in the actual production of the products and services. The challenge for the company is now to understand the customers' processes: when, where, how, and why they do things, and where we as a company fit into the process. Richard Normann at SMG has been a pioneer in the research and understanding of the customer as co-producer of services.

In cafeterias, we serve ourselves (and tidy up afterwards if we're at McDonald's), we stand outside the bank's cash machine in the rain and produce the services that were previously carried out by cashiers, and IKEA has taught us to assemble our own furniture. The customer is not only a passive receiver of products and services – a consumer – but an active participant who creates the services and products – a producer. Nowadays the idea of the customer as a co-producer is well anchored since we are expected to do ever more of the work ourselves on the internet; everything from internet banking to booking our own plane tickets. The customer becomes part of the company. He/she ends up on the same side of the equation as the company and becomes a partner in the production process:

Company + Customer = Service or Product

However, the insight that the customer together with the company creates the service is not, in my opinion, enough to explain today's customer. The customer as 'co-producer' implies that he/she is a 'receiver' or a 'source', that the customer is on one side and the company on the other. What is happening now is that the company and the customer are becoming one.

I would describe my own value chain for the interactive company as:

Customer = Company

The customer is part of the company. The company is part of the customer, and thereby the customer and company become one and the same. And I would revert back to the description of the customer with the harder term, *user*. On the web, we often speak of users; someone uses your website in a similar way to someone using an electric drill. The drill is an extension of the user's arm. The drill does not have a customer, it has a user. The manufacturing company Black & Decker has the customer.

Ericsson ran an advertising campaign with the theme 'Make yourself heard.' The company becomes part of the user and they fuse together to give the person the capacity to communicate globally, irrespective of time and place.

Web companies take on the customers' perspective of the world. This is the new view. The old view can be illustrated by the image of an automobile company: a factory in the middle and customers surrounding it. This is the company's view of its world; ourselves in the middle, and out there a market where we can sell our products to customers with whom we have relationships. This company may see the customer as a co-producer or a 'partner' or whatever it wants to. Either way the customer is someone who is outside and someone you sell things to.

> THERE IS A BIG DIFFERENCE BETWEEN BEING USER FRIENDLY AND BEING A USER, BETWEEN BEING CUSTOMER FOCUSED AND BEING A CUSTOMER

I prefer marketplaces selling cars on the internet. Here, the view is the opposite: a user in the middle who gets a tool to help them choose one of the car brands on offer. This is the customer's real perspective. At Fondex the idea was similar – a marketplace for mutual funds – to see the world through the eyes of the user. Instead of having our own products, we gathered everyone else's products in one place and the web became the tool at the disposal of the customers. Of course, this is especially true for consumer companies.

Companies boast about being user friendly and customer focused. However, there is a big difference between being user friendly and being a user, between being customer focused and being a customer.

Marshall McLuhan described the wheel as an extension of the foot, clothes as an extension of the skin, TV as an extension of the eye – and the internet (although it wasn't called that then) as an extension of the neural system. A website or any digital interface or tool is, in a similar way, an extension of the user. Isn't your mailbox part of you?

The drill is the extension of the part of the body needed to perform a specific task. In the same way, a web company – the whole company, since it is a service company – is a tool for the user. It puts all its resources at the disposal of the customer who wants to carry out a function or a task. This is even clearer on websites where users can personalize the content to suit themselves; at the internet broker Schwab, there is My Schwab, at Yahoo! you have My Yahoo! and Netscape offers My Netscape.

> **"** The customer is no longer only part of the company, the company is also part of the user. And all the company's resources, ideas, knowledge, and assets are manifested in this interface that is the user's tool. Start to see your company as a tool, if you don't already do so. **"**

To think human

If the idea economy is about experimenting, the web is about being clear and concise. Finding ideas is an unpredictable, chaotic business; running a business on the web is about predictable structure. You may experiment as much as you like within the company – and you should! – but in your digital window to the world, be pedantically neat and tidy. The larger part of the technical investments in e-commerce businesses is spent on building trading systems and databases. But the surface symbolizes that the systems actually work.

At one of the Fondex suppliers, I put up a large poster on the wall which read: 'Think Web!' When they had programmed in some rather odd interface for order placement, I asked them to go down on to the street, pick a stranger (for it is strangers we work with on the web), bring them upstairs, sit them in front of the computer and let that person from the real world use the system. This tests whether the system really works or not. Thinking web is not primarily about technology.

Thinking web means to think in terms of the person using the web or the actual digital service that you offer. Thinking web is to think human.

We breathe – this is a natural interaction with nature. We walk up a flight of stairs – this is interaction with the manufactured world. The stairs are efficient and well designed if the steps are the right height and the right length. I would like to see design as our interaction with the manufactured world. Whether we sit in front of a website or on a sofa, design is what we experience. Design becomes all the more important since we interact more and more with machines. Most of the time, design risks getting in the way. But at its best, it helps the company and its products and services become part of the user.

To meet the people you never meet – the users

The sad part of running an e-commerce business is that you hardly ever meet real customers. A shop on the high street leads to unique direct contact with customers. Your website, on the other hand, reaches millions of computers, but you never meet your users when they are shopping, you don't know what they look like or what they are thinking or what they think of you. Sure, there is some communication via customer services, but there is usually no deeper contact. You can feel a bit lonely.

Since you don't get to meet your customers in a natural manner, you have to find 'artificial' ways to meet them, ways that resemble reality as much as possible. These meetings tend to be called user tests, but I prefer to call them user meetings. You invite real users to user meetings and ask them to perform real tasks. Real users performing real tasks is the only real way to test a website.

The users can be invited from your own database or they can be screened with the help of telephone interviews. The meeting normally consists of a group of 8 to 10 people who are asked to carry out approximately 10 tasks on the website: for example purchasing something, registering as a customer or getting hold of some information. You are present when the users perform these tasks and afterwards during the discussion.

Try to work with two groups, for example, one with men and one with women. Or mixed groups but of different ages. In this way you can learn something about the differences that exist from one user group to another.

One example of a function that is worth testing by a user group is the registration function. This is an area where you can fail miserably. What you want to achieve with the registration is to convert visitors on the website to registered customers. The opposite is often the result and visitors stop and turn back when forced to leave a name and address.

The registration has to be simple and take as little time as possible. But you also have to understand intrinsically what this entails. What is the logical sequence when registering? Which words should be used? Should you call it member registration or customer registration? Do your users feel like customers or members? If you have to leave personal or sensitive information, does the registration form need to explain why? When the registration is complete and the user is about to send the information back, which word inspires most confidence – 'Send,' 'Submit,' 'Confirm' or 'OK?' If the response time for downloading the information into the database exceeds 10 seconds, what is happening while the customer is waiting?

The quality on a website, or any other digital interface, be it a phone or a Personal Digital Assistant, is determined by the smallest level of detail. It is not sufficient to establish that the general quality is good. The best interfaces are successful with the specific. Thinking web is to understand the details in digital communication.

Another way of finding out what users think is to carry out telephone interviews or to send out questionnaires. During a telephone interview, you can ask a user what they would like to see on the website. With questionnaires sent out in the post, you can ask the recipient to get on to the internet and on to your site and ask them to comment on the content. Quantitative market research can give a superficial picture of what your users think and feel. It can be useful as a basis for qualitative research, but there is only one real way to really understand the web – to meet real users who carry out real tasks. (This is something that has also been corroborated by the web guru Jacob Nielsen.)

"Remember that you yourself are a real user. One way to understand the web is to use it in your daily life and reflect on how you use it.

Organize user meetings at least once every quarter. Not only should user focus be a living part of your culture, but as the website is constantly changing, new ideas need to be tested.

If you want to know what to do with your own website, surf around on others and see what they have done. Find a list of the world's, say, 30 best companies on the web. Look at how they present themselves on their first page, where they put their navigation tools and how they have solved customer registration. If you see a pattern that works, do the same! And you should adapt your site to standards so the users themselves learn to recognize such patterns.

You are not rewarded for original design but for functionality."

The dialog with the users

The dialog with the users is a cornerstone in a web culture. A company never has enough knowledge to develop the best website and that's why you should ask the users. They often have questions of a concrete nature and everything needs to be crystal clear. Here are some examples from a user meeting I attended.

User comments	My notes
'Try Fondex free' sounds as if it costs something later on.	It is free. But the customers will think that they have to pay up later.
When registering, I did not understand the difference between subscriber, member or customer.	Customers don't care about which type of user they are, they care about what they get.
I noticed a spelling mistake, which felt worrying.	This is just as bad as if the entrance to the bank had a vandalized door.
In the FAQ section, you can only see 20 questions at a time. Of how many thousand ...	Users want to see the whole and then choose from it. It must be predictable.
It should say 'Contact us' instead of just 'Contact', and 'Guide' instead of 'Map.'	They thought map meant directions to the office when it was a map of the website.

During this user meeting we had two groups: existing customers and users that had not visited our site previously. The result showed that there was no significant difference in the opinions of the two groups. Both were equally confused. It struck me that not even our own customers really understood how the whole thing actually worked. But they had become customers anyway. I thought about all those we had lost just because we had not succeeded in being clear enough.

The users at this meeting liked the content and the information, but there was a lot in the way. They wanted to get straight to the interesting bit. It was unclear what Fondex really did, how much it cost, how you purchased and how you registered.

The users want to feel safe on a website where they deposit their money. A lack of clarity creates a feeling of insecurity, and insecurity reduces trust.

The best way to create trust is simplicity and predictability. Predictability creates security. 'Boring' means secure. An e-commerce company ultimately

"THE BEST WAY TO CREATE TRUST IS SIMPLICITY AND PREDICTABILITY"

wants their customers to feel so safe and bored that they become lazy, i.e. do more and more business on the web.

This time, the user meeting led to five concrete changes. The website was tidied up and became clearer. A description of what you get as a customer and how the company works was added to the front page. 'Free' was explained better. The registration function was changed, as was the member/customer/subscriber terminology. Wording and spelling was checked and corrected throughout the website.

66 Everything can be simplified. Make it as simple as possible. And then make it even simpler.

And then even simpler. And simpler still. And finally, simplify again. Don't be afraid to simplify.

Downsize. To then upsize. 99

Customer service

The image I have of how a company should be organized is a big room and in the middle of the room you find customer service. In this way, customers and users physically become the central part of the business. This is how we organized customer service at Fondex: I could never leave my desk and walk to the entrance without passing through customer service and it became impossible not to be part of the constant dialog with the customers.

Another principle is that customer service should not be restricted to one department of the company. Everyone is customer service. Those who work with technology do technology support. The editorial team answer news questions. Marketing answer marketing questions. No one has the right to be shut off from the customers.

Lars Stahre, the man behind the website of the Swedish business daily *Dagens Industri*, di.se, has been a source of inspiration for me. It is by far one of Sweden's largest financial services on the web. Lars personally handled a lot of the customer service. And it really is personal. When we met, he was usually running around *DI*'s newsdesk with a constantly ringing mobile phone, answering the most diverse questions, from members wondering why the internet was slow at seven o'clock that morning, to those who were on their way to Stockholm wanting a recommendation of what restaurant to eat at. Lars made me realize that customer service is the best way to understand what the users want and it is a deadly sin to outsource customer service or isolate it within the company. At Fondex we looked into the possibility of using a call center for handling calls but we chose to take care of all customer service ourselves. The users helped the company to understand its business.

66 Develop the dialog with your users, they will teach you a lot. How can a company with 10 employees be smarter than 100,000 users? 99

You've got mail

In a company with internet-literate customers, you normally receive more e-mail than telephone calls. There are three things to say about customer service via e-mail:

- Prompt answers are an unbeatable way of quickly gaining goodwill.
- It generally takes longer to answer via e-mail than it does on the phone.
- Communication via e-mail can always be made more efficient.

When journalists test web services they usually send an e-mail to the company and see how long it takes to get a reply. The faster the reply, the higher the credibility (and better PR for the company). Long response times = nonprofessional. Customers think in the same way. A fast response via e-mail is not only a sign of fast service, it is also proof that there is somebody on the other side. How many times have you sent a question to a web company via the 'Contact us' button and wondered whether you'll ever get an answer? Getting an answer is a positive surprise, getting an answer fast is the start of a human relationship that creates trust and goodwill.

It generally takes longer to answer via e-mail than it does to speak over the phone since e-mail is written communication and is more time-consuming. E-mail also tends to give rise to follow-on questions, which means another round of communication. On the telephone, problems can be solved faster since communication is in real time and is more subtle than the concise language of e-mail. Hence, communicating by e-mail should not always be the obvious choice for a company.

One advantage with e-mail is that a certain level of automation can be created. After a while, the company begins to recognize certain questions that are asked over and over again and a number of standardized answers can be set up. An efficient customer service via e-mail is based upon a bank of ready answers. This part of the operation can even be outsourced.

One rule of thumb is that roughly 80 percent of the questions sent to customer service are repeat questions. The other 20 percent are more unusual and it is these that can provide useful insights for the company.

People to people

All costs related to customer service are an investment in goodwill and building trust. It is also a type of cost that is hard to make more efficient on the internet, despite voice-controlled computers and experiments with artificial intelligence that can make a machine answer incoming queries. People are needed to take care of people.

At the beginning of 2000, AOL had approximately 12,000 employees and some 22 million customers. Amazon.com had nearly 8,000 employees and around 17 million customers. The internet trader E-Trade had over 1,000 employees and some two million customer accounts. Although there is no scientific evidence to support this, you could say that there is a ratio of one employee to every 2,000 customers in a large e-commerce company. In smaller companies, the ratio may be different and there are usually fewer customers per employee. What you want to achieve is as few employees as possible, with a maximum number of customers and a growing transaction value per customer.

It is, at the same time, difficult to keep costs under control. In a growing business, the number of employees grows, partly because the web company has to have the best customer service in order to be competitive with respect to its physical counterparts – the shops on the high street – and partly because the business itself is new and thereby needs to give its customers extra support. Despite obtaining economies of scale in technology, where many can be served simultaneously via a website, there is a tendency to take care of customers one at a time.

All new recruits in a web company are certainly not directly involved in customer service, but with time, it becomes one of the single largest costs.

66 Web-based business is isolated since you never meet the users. And the users never meet you, except via digital screens. Customer service is one of the few channels open to your customers and is therefore of great importance. 99

Your trust manager
Trust is a killer application. Leading up to the millennium, and the millennium bug that was feared by many (which didn't amount to anything in the end), companies and authorities erected signs declaring that the systems had been checked for Y2K problems. The Swedish government made it their mission to control, rectify and certify all public computer systems and award them with a quality stamp, rather like the marking of environmentally friendly household goods, so that we, the consumers, would know that the systems were Y2K safe.

Companies need symbols of trust. At the beginning of 2000, we created a new job description and role at Fondex. We called it the Trust Manager.

A Trust Manager's job is to create trust by making the company feel more secure. This person has to be a customer and has to use the website daily and think about the website from an external perspective.

Working at a web company means taking responsibility for everything that leaves the company and for every surface on which the company can be seen. Responsibility for delivering what has been promised, for the systems being up and running, for the shop being open, and for a high level of service. In a web culture, everyone is responsible for the website, but a Trust Manager symbolizes the values and is the recipient of views, comments and suggestions for improvement.

Fondex had a weekly meeting where views were discussed and changes were made. Changes and ideas were delegated to the project leader and the webmaster who have between one and five days to make the change, depending on its scope. Larger changes were made into separate projects which were given individual budgets.

There was also a Head of Customer Services at Fondex, but that was an entirely different role. Customer Service took care of customers in need of personal support and guidance. Perhaps orders needed to be followed up, a fax needed sending or a complaint needed dealing with. Customer Service was, in its nature, reactive. They handled, approximately, 5 to 10 percent of all customers. The remainder never contacted us and the only contact we had with them was via our web interface, WAP telephones, news sent out to their Palm Pilots, electronic messages and weekly newsletters.

Trust on the web is built in each moment that you interact with your users, each time someone types www.your-web.com, each time a new page is downloaded, each time you send out an e-mail or text to a mobile phone. Every spelling mistake is a minus in the profit and loss statement because you risk losing a potential customer whose trust you did not gain. Business on the web is about details. Customer service used to be a 24-hour service, today it's about answering an e-mail in 24 seconds.

> **"** CUSTOMER SERVICE USED TO BE A 24-HOUR SERVICE, TODAY IT'S ABOUT ANSWERING AN E-MAIL IN 24 SECONDS **"**

In every contact opportunity trust is created for the company. When Scandinavian Airlines (SAS) went through its service revolution in the 1980s, the expression 'moment of truth' was used to describe the challenge ahead, namely that each time a passenger meets an SAS employee, the whole company is judged. The former CEO for SAS, Jan Carlzon, later wrote a book with the same name, *Moment of Truth.*

There is a lot of clarity in personal, face-to-face contact in a physical environment at, for example, a check-in desk at an airport. The context is clear, the roles are clear and the communication is interactive, real-time. The dialog consists not only of words but also of facial expressions, gestures, documents that are handled, the color of the employee's uniform (with a clear name badge) and the passenger's bonus card. People are good at communicating with all their senses and are used to using their senses to create an overall impression, which makes the communication effective. Uniform = trust. Pleasant smell = order. Nice smile = service. Good verbal approach = professionalism. Gold card = VIP.

On the web, the scope for expression is very limited and the moments of contact are more intense. The communication often flows in one direction. You usually don't know with whom you are communicating. Not only your customers, but practically anybody may be looking at your website.

The moment of truth is extreme in web companies. Therefore, your Trust Manager needs to take a proactive approach. It is about taking care of and cultivating the surface which is the web company's interface with the outside world and where the company is judged at every individual encounter. It is about building trust with all the users that never contact Customer Services, who are anonymous and make their own judgment of the company from the surface, which is often the only part of the company they will ever see. A Trust Manager cares about the surface.

Some principles that a Trust Manager should work from:

- *Information for information.* We know that most people today go to a certain website because it contains useful information. The first transaction at a web company is information for information – a new visitor thinks our information is so good they want to register. Or expressed in another way: pay for our information by supplying information about yourself.

- *No transaction without a relationship.* Good relationships in the provision of information can be transformed into good relationships in the provision of transaction services. This is especially the case with financial consumer services which is an industry built on trust. Trust is built on good relationships.

- *The website should save more than it costs.* The benefit and value of the experience on a website must be greater than the time a user spends on it. Otherwise a benefit deficit occurs.

Four seconds
A web company has to be able to acquire and serve customers via the web. A lack of clarity and 'user unfriendliness' are two of the largest obstacles for getting customers. Users expect useful websites.

Experienced users can't be bothered with bad websites and beginners turn back if they don't understand where they are. Users prefer to visit sites they are familiar with rather than spending time learning something new.

New services must therefore be easy to understand and offer superior benefits over already existing services. But it is also human nature to question why we should do something we've never done before.

I like to think that you have approximately four seconds to persuade a user that you have something to offer them on your website; one second to give a first impression and three seconds to tell them who you are.

Well-known brands, clear design and simple texts help. Otherwise you risk losing the user via the merciless back-button on the web browser.

Thresholds are already high in web-based businesses since users are naturally sceptical, pressed for time, and wonder why they should care in the first place. A bad interface will increase the threshold even more. But a well-designed interface gives you an opportunity to lower the threshold. New websites with new business ideas and original services must have extremely good interfaces in order to succeed. Users normally can't be bothered to take the time to get to know a new website. They want to get directly down to business and use it if it seems good.

Welcome to the factory You thought you'd left the industrial era and entered the new economy, didn't you? Perhaps. But a good website is actually very similar to a factory, being process driven. What many production companies spent time doing during the 1900s in order to increase productivity – process management – fits the web too.

Process management is basically about exploring every part of a business and then making the parts more efficient in order to increase productivity. This is important in a factory and on the web.

" USERS NORMALLY CAN'T BE BOTHERED TO TAKE THE TIME TO GET TO KNOW A NEW WEBSITE. THEY WANT TO GET DIRECTLY DOWN TO BUSINESS AND USE IT IF IT SEEMS GOOD "

I believe that process management dampens creativity in companies since the focus is on measuring and trimming the existing instead of developing the new. However, a web company cannot only live on creating new ideas, it must also understand the logistics and structure in the underlying business.

A key activity in an e-commerce company is to organize the flows: the flow of traffic from users, product flows from suppliers and payment flows. The central point for the flows is the website (from the user's perspective), even though from a logistical point of view it may be handled in a warehouse or a back office.

A user who becomes a customer goes through a process in the company's interface, and it is important to get organized around this process. Think web! It's wrong to force users to adapt themselves to your company's own processes, which is often the case when established companies move out onto the web.

Depending on the industry, the user's process on the web will differ. At a web-based book store, the process might look like this: User searches for product information, chooses a book, goes to the checkout, registers, pays with a credit card, is informed of the delivery method, and one week later the book comes in the post.

A financial consumer service has a different pattern. Here, a written contract is needed before you can become a customer and start trading. After this, the trading and all other services are handled completely digitally. The financial factory is a process comprising of five main steps:

one   Visitor arrives at the website where the services and special offers are presented.

two   Visitors who want to become customers register.

three   Company sends a written contract in the post and the account is opened when the customer has signed the contract and sent the papers back to the company.

four   Customers transfer money and funds to their account.

five   Customers log into their account, buy and sell funds and stocks, follow the development of their portfolio, and make use of the tools and information services in order to maximize investments.

A company on the web has two main user groups: customers and potential customers. New visitors must easily be able to carry out steps 1–4 and customers must easily be able to carry out the loop 4–5. Many new and returning visitors remain at step 1 for a long time without our knowing who they are; they are only picked up as traffic. Often, they do not proceed any further.

Everything in an internet business is about supporting the customers-development process by reaching potential customers, having appealing offers and an effective website. The web should support the process, not hinder it. However, it is often difficult for a company to even get past step 1 – describing who you are and what you have to offer. The challenge is to get the user to move on and use the tool.

Six months after launching the Fondex website, we had fairly high traffic figures, but few registered customers. At each user testing occasion, one question always came up 'What's in it for me?' This was a question we had failed to answer. In other words, we had a website that was counterproductive in the first step of the business process. Having done several user tests, we found a solution that was almost embarrassingly obvious:

We must explain what the company is.

We must explain what you get as a customer.

We must explain how you can register easily.

We must explain what happens after that.

It doesn't matter which company you are talking about, the first steps are always the same. But it is easy to forget to answer the simplest of questions: who you are, what you offer, and how to become a customer.

“The web is direct. In building a business on the internet, always take the most direct route.

Why do people come to your website? Begin by presenting yourself and what you have to offer. ”

Click here!
Interactive communication, maybe, but using the web is remarkably similar to flicking though a catalog. If the user likes the content, the foundations are laid for a deeper, interactive communication where the user and the website begin to exchange information of a more intimate nature and the relationship may develop into customer and salesperson. Interactivity has been established and it no longer resembles the traditional catalog. The prerequisite is that the web succeeds in communicating at step one, otherwise there is no continued contact.

“NEVER LET THE FORM OBSCURE THE FUNCTION. THINK SMS: NOT MUCH DESIGN, BUT MILLIONS OF DAILY USERS ”

Never let the form obscure the function. Think text messages or e-mail: not much design, but millions of daily users. Why? Because it's simple and effective. It is an information service that delivers. Much on the web never gets to be half as effective as text or e-mail.

One of the world's largest web companies, the search engine Yahoo!, is a company with the world's ugliest design. In reality, there is no design at all, it is 100 percent function. In most cases, this is exactly how it should be. Dare to be simple.

Being simple is not just about having simple graphic solutions, it is also about expressing yourself clearly in texts. So far, the web and many other digital services are text-based media, and a lot of our interactive world will for some time continue to be text-based, such as text messages to mobile phones, e-mail and HTML text on the web. In many ways, the internet is the renaissance of the written word, or it should be. Those who use e-mail learn how to express themselves concisely in order to avoid misunderstandings.

On the web, you find unclear texts and instructions all too often, not least when it comes to purchasing and where to put the money. The same thing applies to texts as to design – do not overcomplicate. The result can only be inferior. Texts should be concise and clear, with one message at a time. The most effective text that was ever invented on the web is the classic 'Click here!' with the link underlined in blue. It is hard to misunderstand. Do you think this is banal? There are people who love simplicity: the users.

But watch out! The web is no place for technocratic and callous robotic language. If we were only met by cold sentences like 'Click here!' on every page, we would soon lose heart. Companies on the internet must be like nice restaurants: guests feel at home with the other guests, the service is good, and the food tasty. Otherwise they will not return. Today, too many companies adhere more to the school dinners principle: fairly practical, but as soon as you have finished your meal, you want to get out of the dining room.

The web is about interaction and communication – and just like in the rest of the world, it helps to be nice. Be polite and the world becomes a nicer place. On the web, you can never use the following words often enough:

66 THE WEB IS ABOUT INTERACTION AND COMMUNICATION – AND JUST LIKE IN THE REST OF THE WORLD, IT HELPS TO BE NICE **99**

WELCOME (to us, this is us, and we will take care of you in the best possible way)

PLEASE (leave your name and address before you purchase)

THANK YOU (for wanting to register your address).

THANK YOU for wanting to read these lines! I appreciate that you are investing your time in my book which I hope will create more value for you than it cost you to buy it.

PLEASE feel free to contact me at any time. Click here! Think web.

Not the latest technology – but the simplest
Technical development could be summarized like this: it's complicated enough anyway. That is to say, always use the simplest technology; it's complicated enough

anyway. New technology is developed every day. This is as true as the fact that those who work with technology like to work with new technology. And the better you are, the newer the technology you want to work with. Does that mean that the best programmers always work with the best technology? Perhaps, perhaps not. But what I have learned is that the simplest technology is often the best technology. The latest technology, on the other hand, is seldom the most appropriate technology.

The reason that technical projects often end up complicated is due to the large number of variables and alternatives involved. Programming language, technical platforms, different architecture, software and hardware, all quickly turn into a fairly complex labyrinth.

Take the following example. The world consists of both Mac and PC. The world is also made up of different browsers such as Microsoft Explorer and Netscape Navigator. Furthermore, the world is made up of different versions of the browsers Explorer and Navigator, that is versions 1.0, 2.0, 3.0, 4.0, 5.0, and so on. Two different types of computers, and two different browsers in five different versions give $2 \times 2 \times 5 = 20$ different combinations. The problem with this is that a web page often looks different depending on which combination of computer, browser and version a user is using. But the simpler the technology, the greater the chance that the page works in any combination.

Among other things, that is why Yahoo! looks like it does – in order that as many people as possible are able to use the website. Yahoo! has millions of unique users per month – many would be pissed off if they couldn't read what was on the page. For the same reason Amazon instructs its programmers to construct the site so that it works for a version 1.0 browser, despite the fact that this version is outdated. I have tried, and you can actually buy books from Amazon from an old Mosaic browser from 1994. It doesn't look good, but it works. Use simple technology. And sleep well.

CHAPTER SEVEN

Business: To do the new thing

7

THE ONLY SCARCITY IN A WORLD OF ABUNDANCE

IS HUMAN ATTENTION

KEVIN KELLY, NEW ECONOMY WRITER

New services to new customers

Consumers are exposed to more and more advanced product and service offerings from both new and old companies: games on mobile phones, Japanese index funds, web auctions for Christmas trees, 24-hour stock trading, online banking at the grocery, websites for sending birthday e-mails. The average consumer is getting fairly well educated in being a consumer and so can understand more and more complex product or service offerings. However, the consumer may be getting very tired.

The more 'educated' you are, the larger the experience and benefit – and the larger the experience and benefit, the more you are willing to pay. A wine lover is willing to pay for a bottle of Château Margaux, and the opera lover will gladly spend a thousand dollars on good seats at La Scala in Milan. The motivation for companies to educate its own customers in the products and services it offers is huge. A user who is 'educated' in how a certain website works, thereby feeling like an experienced user, is more likely to be a customer than their less-educated counterpart. Knowledge tends to inspire self-confidence. (Demos and guides on a website therefore tend to be good investments.)

It follows that a very simple service makes things easier, like Hotmail, for example, compared to a complex web service that is difficult to explain. If the service is new on the market, the company behind the service has to have a large educational budget, i.e. marketing.

Both new and old companies spend a lot of time on serious business development, and it seems as though this development has its origins in 'Isn't this something that everyone would like …'

I'm the first to admit that one of the most important characteristics for economic development is the ability to waste time and money and resources in order to come up with something new. When Sony launched the Walkman in the mid-1970s, there was not one consumer who had asked for a tape recorder that you could only listen to and not use for recording. When consumers saw the product, they said 'Aha.'

❝ THE AHA FACTOR IS A PREREQUISITE FOR BEING ABLE TO LAUNCH NEW IDEAS TO CUSTOMERS ❞

When Hotmail was launched in 1996, after entrepreneurs and venture capitalists had invested significant amounts of time, money and resources in this new thing that no one had asked for, consumers said 'Aha, free email, accessed through the internet …' Three years later, Hotmail had over 50 million registered users. Nobody had requested mobile operator Comviq's refillable telephone card for mobile phones, but when the card came on to the Swedish market, hundreds of thousands of consumers said 'Aha …' The aha-factor is a prerequisite for being able to launch new ideas to customers.

There are two ground rules when it comes to successful product development on a consumer market:

- It must be simple.
- Many must want it, sooner or later.

How do you know if any idea is simple? An idea is often simple if it can be explained in a simple way. If you can't explain your business in a couple of words, it's usually not worth pursuing further. The fact that an idea is simple does not make it unqualified, rather the opposite. It is often the case that the simpler the idea, the more advanced is the technology behind it.

How do you know that many will want your idea? Find out by answering these tough questions:

- Does the idea have aha-potential?
- Do customers understand your idea?
- Do they have time for your idea?
- Do they want to pay for it?
- And even if they do, will they change their habits and move for your sake?

And how do you get an answer to all this? By doing.

To do the right thing right

It is much better to do the right thing the wrong way, than to do the wrong thing the right way. In the mid-1990s, Swedish insurance giant Trygg-Hansa was moving out on to the web with their campaign 'Life's Department Store.' The problem was that the website contained so many pictures and graphics that few people actually managed to get on to the site with the slow modems at that time, and the company's website was renamed by consumers as 'Life's Waiting Room.'

> **IT IS MUCH BETTER TO DO THE RIGHT THING THE WRONG WAY, THAN TO DO THE WRONG THING THE RIGHT WAY**

But this was not a failure, quite the opposite. Trygg-Hansa may have gone about things the wrong way, but it was the right thing to do. A couple of years later when Trygg-Hansa launched their new website, they had learned from their mistakes and did the right thing the right way with a fast and informative internet service. This is an example of an idea culture producing a competitive edge.

How companies respond to change:

Doing the wrong thing, the right way	Doing the right thing, the right way
Doing the wrong thing, the wrong way	Doing the right thing, the wrong way

Yahoo! started to build a simple search engine just as the traffic on the internet started increasing. They did the right thing. And they also did it the right way, with a simple interface and an effective and scalable database technology that became a trend setter. However, few companies do the right things the right way straight away.

A financial company that is having trouble finding its way on the net is the Swedish bank Handelsbanken. They have successfully built a profitable and decentralized banking organization, but found themselves in a dilemma when it was time to build up a website. The internet is a place where distances no longer exist, and yet visitors to Handelsbanken's internet bank were asked to decide first and foremost which local branch they belonged to. Instead of rethinking, Handelsbanken chose to think along the lines that they had always done, which I think is an example of doing the wrong thing, though it was in the right way from their culture's point of view.

Another example of doing the wrong thing the right way is when internet companies spend millions of dollars on marketing with proper advertising campaigns in order to achieve a strong brand name. That is the wrong thing. What you want is to build a large customer base, which is the right thing.

"A common problem for companies in fast-moving markets is that new questions often get old answers. You are doing things, but it's the wrong things. Try to be on the right track, even though you may make some mistakes on the way."

Wasting time

There are two fundamental principles of innovation. The first is 'Necessity is the mother of invention.' This proverb, translated to the downsizing, restructuring, and business process that re-engineered the economies of the early 1990s, meant trimming, saving and developing to be constantly better, more efficient and more productive. Yet companies such as Nokia and Ericsson state that the largest source of profitability for the coming years will be from products that are as yet unknown. What is already known can be produced by anyone. The profits lie in the unknown, the new. The dilemma is that the new, by definition, cannot be planned. All that can be done is to create an environment for new ideas and hope that you find the right ones.

There are four different standard situations in a market:

- You deliver what you have and what the customers want, like milk.
- You sell what you have but what the customers don't yet know they need, like a new pensions saving scheme.
- You listen to customers to find out what they want and then develop a product that didn't exist before, like environmentally friendly detergent.
- Neither the customers nor you know what the need is.

In this not-too-uncommon final situation you follow the second principle of innovation. It's called 'wasting time.' This is about using up resources in order to find new ideas. Investing in areas that are not yet mapped out without knowing the return. Backing projects and ideas without knowing where they are heading, at least not according to established rules.

66 When you can't tell which is the right or wrong thing to do, there is only one way to go: do the

thing you believe in. This is never wrong. 99

Pricing on the net
We know more or less what a pint of milk or a bus fare ought to cost, but on the internet, there are no obvious prices. Pricing is

one of the biggest mysteries in business, and especially for new services like digital media. How do you charge? And for what? Pricing new digital media has traditionally revolved around two central phenomena, which I call relative pricing and alternative sources of income.

Relative pricing

With relative pricing, one product can cost one thing in one place, while it costs less or is offered free somewhere else in an effort to attract customers. The price is what a buyer is willing to pay for a product or service, and this is often determined by what it costs elsewhere, and the fact that a buyer normally wants to pay as little as possible. The typical example is the web bookstore that attracts customers from the bookstore on the high street by offering lower prices.

The fundamental principle behind relative pricing is cost efficiency, i.e. a web company, for example, can run its operations at lower costs and can therefore cut margins. However, it is often at least as expensive, if not much more so, to run a technically complex e-commerce operation with losses on each item sold, which in turn can mean that the more the company sells, the larger the losses. A company that builds its business on relative pricing needs to analyze the product and cash flows realistically beforehand. Usually, revenues are overestimated and costs underestimated.

> **"RELATIVE PRICING IS OFTEN USED AGGRESSIVELY IN ORDER TO BUILD A CUSTOMER BASE OR MARKET SHARE"**

Relative pricing is often used aggressively in order to build a customer base or market share. On the internet, you hear people saying that one company's revenue model is just another company's customer base strategy. The typical example was telephone operators selling internet subscriptions who suddenly got competition from new operators offering free internet access.

The price is what a buyer is willing to pay for a product or service and it is hard to charge for what can be found free elsewhere. Today, hardly anybody pays for standard internet access.

Alternative sources of income

Alternative sources of income refer to companies offering one service but getting paid for something else, often by someone other than the person using the service. The typical example is Hotmail, offering free e-mail to the user but getting paid through advertising. Yahoo! works in the same way: the search engine is free but the revenues come from those who buy advertising space. A more refined and nowadays classic example is Netscape, who built its business by giving its browser away free on the internet to consumers in an effort to build a market, and then get paid for servers and software from e-commerce businesses.

Another example of alternative sources of income are the marketplaces on the internet. Intermediaries, where you can choose telephone subscriptions, insurance, cars, and mutual funds, are often free for the user since the marketplaces get their revenues from delivering customers to the various sellers advertised on your site. The marketplaces, like many other companies that are active on the internet, offer consumer services on the surface but they get their revenues from business customers. The business lies in creating traffic and converting it into revenue flows.

Alternative sources of revenue are something that consumers have come to understand: I get to use this service free of charge as the company earns its money some other way. This has in turn led to consumers understanding that there are many ways they can pay for services on the internet. For example:

- money
- information
- time
- traffic.

You can pay in the traditional way by obtaining a product or service in exchange for money: you reserve a plane ticket and give them your credit card number.

Users can also pay with information about themselves, for example, by 'paying' with their e-mail address and in exchange receiving a weekly electronic newsletter.

We live in a culture of waiting. You wait on average two minutes while booting up the computer. You wait five minutes to access the internet. You wait for pictures to download. You wait for something on the television. What do you do while you are waiting? Some companies pay us for spending our waiting time looking at advertisements, in the way that we pay for a movie on TV by looking at the ads during the break.

Traffic is related to the time payment method. I pay for a web service by surfing on the site. Each time you download a page from your favorite newspaper on the web, the paper earns a few cents through banner exposure.

66 Customers and users are usually aware of how they are paying for a service, like advertisement-paid TV or a free paper. But with many new business ideas on the internet, it is not always obvious who is paying and how. This can create uncertainty. Explain in a clear way where your company gets its revenues from. 99

Value-based pricing
There is a third pricing model, which I call value-based pricing. This is the best and probably also the oldest form of pricing – you get paid for the value of the product or the service. The problem with the internet is that it creates true user value, but it is very hard to get paid for it.

Compare this to mobile phones. It costs roughly $0.5 per minute to make national calls and over $1 to call abroad. If you are in Hong Kong and call

Stockholm, it costs some $10 per minute. Do you call less as a result? No. Why? Because you can't go without. The price equals the value of the service.

You are in London. Imagine it cost you 50 pence to send an e-mail to Liverpool, £1 to Paris, and £5 to Hong Kong. Would you send it? Probably yes, because it's quick, reliable, and effective. It is worth the cost, motivated by the benefit. You would probably send less e-mails than you do today, but not that many less. Imagine being an 'e-mail operator' getting paid for each e-mail that is sent. The difference is that mobile phone operators get paid for the benefit, since they own the infrastructure.

Consumers have learned that the internet is cheaper (and often completely free!), and the low prices and opportunity to save money has attracted customers that would perhaps not otherwise have bothered with e-commerce. The low price has been one of the most important catalysts for electronic commerce. In the same way, you could say that subsidized mobile phones, which were often offered practically free of charge, was a way to build a market for mobile telephony.

But a market cannot survive on subsidies in the long run. On the internet, we happily offered services without charging sufficiently for them, dumping prices just to get new customers. That development is a negative spiral on a market because average prices are driven towards zero and consumers learn to expect the services for free. When companies in such a market have gone bankrupt as a result of there no longer being any money to earn, the undermined margins will remain.

When the *Wall Street Journal* started charging for its paper on the internet, it immediately lost around 90 percent of its users. But 10 percent were willing to pay for the benefit they thought the internet paper gave them. Ask yourself this question: What is best, 10 paying customers or 100 free users?

It is hard to charge for content and it is easier to price real services. Internet users do not normally want to pay for what they see, but for what they can

> 66 ON THE INTERNET, WE HAPPILY OFFER SERVICES WITHOUT CHARGING SUFFICIENTLY FOR THEM, DUMPING PRICES JUST TO GET NEW CUSTOMERS 99

do. The internet is still much cheaper, and prices seldom reflect the values that are created for the user.

Companies that want to be successful long term on the web must find user benefits and charge users for these. This is the only way to create lasting profitability. Since the rule of relative pricing says that you cannot get paid for something that is free somewhere else, the long-term successful company must find content and services that are not available anywhere else.

When the global interior company IKEA launched its new website, there was no question of lowering prices on the net. They kept the same prices that they charged in their stores, naturally. With a trusted brand and already low prices, they didn't find that they needed to lower their prices further. IKEA knows exactly what it is doing. They know that they offer their customers good products at very competitive prices and will therefore not lower prices just because the furniture is sold through their website. They argue that the customer value from shopping on the IKEA website is actually even higher than shopping at their stores since it saves time and is more convenient. That's how a very pragmatic company that never bothered much about hype or what others were giving away for free on the internet reasons. IKEA is all about business.

Be unique and personal

The strongest content, which has a unique value that can be priced, is content that is only made available by your company and that is personally adapted to the user.

Within several industries, many similar websites spring up simultaneously. Internet banks, books, CDs, travel agencies, insurance, stocks, and funds are examples of industries where there is a whole array of similar actors fighting for the same pool of customers. The problem is that the internet banks resemble each other, and so do those selling holidays and insurance too. A web company cannot compete long term by offering what is readily available from everyone else and is considered standard. The content for an e-commerce operation should be analyzed from two dimensions:

- Which content and services are accessible to all users, and which are personal?
- Is this content in its turn unique compared to what others offer?

Take a website for trading stocks. There is, for example, information regarding stock prices. This is something that is standard because it is available to all other traders and furthermore it is accessible to all visitors. You can't get paid for standard content (even though you could previously when it was unique). This sort of content can be described as 'standard.'

Say that the company has an editorial team that publishes news on its website, accessible to all. This is unique content that is only available there, but it is accessible to everyone and can therefore not generate revenues. If the site is good, however, it will generate traffic, since users come to the site to use the information (and this traffic can, as you know, be converted into customers). This sort of content can be described as 'traffic driving.'

Like other marketplaces on the web, this company has a system for commerce and trading stocks, which roughly resembles when you fill your shopping basket in a web store and move on to the checkout. These systems are mostly standardized and look the same from one company to the next. Can you differentiate between the checkouts at Tesco from those at Wal-Mart? The only thing the customers expect is that the purchase is quick and efficient. This is 'systems and support.'

Your own pages and your online account at the internet trader are unique since they are only accessible to you. The content is personal: your stock portfolio and how it develops. If the company is smart, other add-on services which cannot be found elsewhere are linked to your account, such as analysis and advice, tools for portfolio allocation and customized news. If these are only available here, they are 'unique and personal' and customers will pay for them.

Companies have to try to produce services and content that are not available anywhere else. Then there is a small chance of being profitable. Exclusivity drives the medium.

The golden rule of openness

In order to achieve long-term competitiveness and profitability, the company must 'lock in' its customers through unique and personal content. This is not about locking up customers, since you do not own your customers, they own themselves. Openness is the golden rule. Which in turn means that if your customers are not satisfied, they will move somewhere else.

Lock-in is about offering such good content that the user wants to stay with you and comes back often and willingly. This is something that TV stations learned a long time ago: the only way to capture flighty viewers is by offering good programmes that are only available on your channel. If changing banks was as easy as zapping from one TV channel to another, banks would be forced to think along these lines too.

> **LOCK-IN IS ABOUT OFFERING SUCH GOOD CONTENT THAT THE USER WANTS TO STAY WITH YOU AND COMES BACK OFTEN AND WILLINGLY**

Banks are a good example of companies trying to lock in customers, by giving out loans, accounts with credit, personal relationships with the bank manager in the local branch, and other ties that are hard to break. It's not unusual to find companies trying their utmost to lock in customers as tightly as possible.

The competitive advantage that banks have had for a long time has been the ability to raise the exit barriers: it's hard to stop being a customer.

Start-ups think very differently since they often start out without a customer base. The competitive advantage here is gained by lowering barriers to entry: registering and becoming a customer has to be easy. Internet companies therefore believe in open markets where customers can move around easily; it means an opportunity for them to capture these customers with outstanding offerings. Internet companies like mobile customers. Established companies normally see this as a threat and a risk of losing existing customers. But no one owns the customers, they own themselves.

In an open environment, even companies like banks would benefit from thinking web, striving for more openness and lowering barriers to entry. Through its local branches, a bank only reaches its existing customers; via the internet, it reaches other banks' customers too.

If you had a website with banner space where companies can advertise, would you accept advertisements from a competitor? Yes, of course. Openness is the key. Users will find their way to the competitor anyway and trying to withhold information is like admitting that you can't compete. You should instead create links to all your competitors on your website so that the users themselves can determine which service is best, and you obviously believe yours is the best. Furthermore, your visitor has probably already added the links to their list of favorites in their browser, so you might as well do the job for them.

> **Companies think on reflex when it comes to competition, lock-in, and protectionism. When openness is spoken of, it is often someone else who needs to become more open. Learn to think of openness as a competitive advantage.**

Marketing is simple, actually

There is an old saying in marketing: half of your investments in marketing are wasted, you just don't know which half. (In e-commerce you sometimes don't have to bother about which half since all marketing investments are wasted money.) Marketing is, however, not as mysterious as it may seem. You need to go about it in a concrete fashion, and we will start with how you do business on the web:

Web business = traffic x conversion rate x transactions

This leads a company, which is looking to build its customer base and to market its products and services, to answer these three questions:

one   how do we achieve traffic?

two   how do we convert traffic to customers?

three   how do we get customers to buy?

This in turn leads to three follow-on questions:

one   which traffic flows? (Who are our customers and where are they? How do we reach them?)

two   which offers? (How do we get them to take the step?)

three   our website? (How do we create a service that they want to use?)

One of the most useful exercises a web company can do is to find out where its potential customers really are. If they read the papers, advertise in the papers. If they travel on the bus, advertise at bus stops. If they surf the economic pages of portals, put up banners there. Do they shop at supermarkets? Do a deal with the supermarkets. Reaching customers is, however, not the same as getting them to act. It is at least as difficult to change behavioral patterns on the internet as it is in the physical world – the people are the same and you don't change your behavior to a greater extent on the web than anywhere else. This means that not many click on banners, and even if they do, there is nothing to say that they will want to become a customer on your website.

Converting traffic to customers is therefore to a large extent about having clear and strong offers. For a long time, lower prices, even free of charge, have been the typical offers. But these not may be enough. Today you have to give the customer more. It's about having a superior website that stimulates visitors to become customers and start doing business. But the internet is actually like direct advertising. Before someone acts, they have to cross the threshold. Reward those who are willing to take the step. And make it easy for them to do so.

Advertising agencies talk a lot about communication, and some call themselves, for want of a clearer identity, communication agencies. On the net, it is not about communicating, it is about selling – hard selling. 'Click here! Win a million!' Being direct is sometimes regarded as vulgar. But on the net, it is rewarded.

And remember, brand awareness is not the same as customer base. You can differentiate between mind share and market share. Mind share is good: you have part of people's attention – they are aware of you. But market share is better: you have a part of the money that an industry turns over. There were many internet companies who became well known quickly without acquiring customers at the same pace. This has been a common problem on the internet. Many know you and about your amazing internet business, but no one cares to become a customer.

> **" THERE ARE MANY INTERNET COMPANIES WHO HAVE BECOME WELL KNOWN QUICKLY WITHOUT ACQUIRING CUSTOMERS AT THE SAME PACE. MANY KNOW YOU, BUT NO ONE WANTS TO BECOME A CUSTOMER "**

At Fondex we noticed an interesting, and maybe frightening, pattern. We could hardly see any difference between the months when we did heavy marketing (TV commercials, printed ads, banner campaigns, etc.) and when we did no marketing at all. The customers just kept on pouring in at a steady but moderate rate. It seemed like marketing just didn't matter and that customers became customers through word of mouth and thanks to recommendations from existing customers. So we started to work on the existing customer base instead, rewarded them for marketing Fondex for us and we got fairly good results.

"You can create a lot of benefits for your users. That's how you create traffic. But if you are not successful at converting traffic into customers and transactions, you do not yet have a web business, only the first step in something that can become a web business (though this can sometimes be valuable enough in itself)."

"Regard marketing practically. It's not really about choosing the slogan for your posters, but about finding your potential customers and offering them benefits."

It's all in the name

On the web, the name and address are the most important components in marketing. Your customers have to be able to find you.

For Fondex, one of the first questions was what the company should be called. It was autumn 1997 and we had planned a launch in October 1998 (it turned out to be May 1999). In other words, we were not in a rush to find a name. But everyone who has managed a project knows that if the project does not have a name, you can't talk about it. Furthermore, the right name can give a hard-to-sell project an unexpected lift if the name is good. There is magic in the right name.

The name Fondex came to me quite quickly. I thought along these lines: the internet is young, cocky and bullish. So this company must have a boring name to create a balance. A hyped-up medium needs a stiff name. Added to the fact that this company was not in the internet industry, it was in the trust industry. I didn't want an internet name, I wanted a safe name. I don't know whether this was the right way of thinking, but it is how I thought.

The name somehow came alive from the start. I may have been the only one who thought the name was good because it was boring. Most of the others liked it because it was distinct, easy to pronounce, easy to remember, and it also explained what business we were in.

Names that describe which business you are in are usually looked down upon as lacking in fantasy by professional communicators and brand experts. But on the net you have to be direct. You never have much time to explain who you are and what you do. There is no time for sophisticated adverts that communicate the 'soul' of your brand. No, the web is about 'cutting the crap.' That is why we have seen many e-commerce companies called such things as etoys.com, eloan.com, wine.com and business.com (the latter was by the way a web address that was sold in January 1999 for nearly $10 million). Tell people who you are, and fast. However, when the market crashes, the domain name will not help much. For example, when the market dived, having a clear name did not help Lastminute.com much.

There are other aspects to a name. It should work in many languages. Yahoo!, Boxman, Boo and Amazon work just as well in Swedish, English, German or French. Sadly, 'Dot Bomb' also became famous globally and Boxman, Boo and others are not around any more.

Need I mention that having the .com address is an advantage when choosing a name? If it is taken, choose another name if you can. Having the .com address is good when, for example, foreign investors read about your company in the *Financial Times* and want to check out your website. Most people try company-name.com first. Dotcom death or not, the .com address is a world standard today.

A friend of mine, internet entrepreneur Alexander Bard, started a company where users can leave their commercial ideas and companies can buy them, if they are good. Call it an exchange for the ideas economy. The company's name is Interesting.org, and they deliberately chose .org because they felt .com was out and because they wanted to underline the business's character-istic as an organization rather than a company.

Choosing a name is one of the most important decisions for a newly started business. The challenge lies in competing in a chaotic landscape where your customers are exposed to thousands of commercial messages each day and where there is a myriad of offers and business ideas. One of your greatest competitive advantages will be clarity. Here is a summary of what you should look for in a good company name:

- simplicity and clarity
- possibility of using the name internationally – it must work in many languages
- rights to internet domains such as .com and .net
- flexible enough not to restrict your activities
- the right feeling – funky or conservative?
- choose a name with star quality.

Creating a hit
When you're setting up a business, or launching a new product or service – there is one question that keeps you awake at night: will it work? You are risking everything, but you have no idea whether it will sell.

We have a lot to learn from the music industry. A gigantic apparatus focused on one single thing: creating hits. A hit is something that everyone knows and that everyone wants.

That is what it is all about, when you are setting up your business and releasing your product or service – creating a hit. On the internet, there was another expression for this phenomenon, namely creating hype around your company. Attention creates expectation and this creates value. Much of internet industry was built on this principle, and in Silicon Valley you can hear the expression 'Hype is the grease on which we slide into the future.' Even though e-commerce failed to live up to much of the hype.

> WHEN YOU'RE SETTING UP A BUSINESS, OR LAUNCHING A NEW PRODUCT OR SERVICE, THERE IS ONE QUESTION THAT KEEPS YOU AWAKE AT NIGHT: WILL IT WORK?

In order to create a hit you need to understand the inner nature of the hit, and besides the music industry, there is probably nowhere better at this than Hollywood. When I think of a hit, I think of one word: *Titanic*, the movie by James Cameron. Why was that a hit? As I see it, a hit is simple, attractive, and has a universal platform.

A product or a service with hit potential is easy to understand, attracts users, and appeals to the needs of many. Pop songs are always simple, with an attractive melody and universal texts. Internet banks are a hit for the same reason. It is easy to do your banking on the web, it is attractive because you don't have to go to the bank, and it is universal – we all need to pay bills. But the real universal aspect, which applies to all of us, is that none of us even wants to think about our bills. The internet banks offer us a quicker way of paying our bills, and thereby reduce the time we have to think about them. Their service is almost as universal as an aspirin, which reduces suffering.

A hit also has a limited shelf life and few companies become classics. If you have created a hit, it normally means that the market will soon lose interest in it and look for the next hit, and the next hit can just as well come from someone else who has a new idea. Therefore, companies must become hit machines that can deliver hit after hit, like Madonna or the Rolling Stones.

In my opinion, the world champion in engineering hits is the Japanese consumer company Sony. In one of their advertisements, you see a young boy wading out into the water by a beach with his back turned towards the onlooker. For his parents, this might be worrying – where is he headed? For the boy, it is a voyage of discovery. The advertisement text is modern poetry of the ideas economy:

He doesn't know what a photograph is
He's never heard of 8-track
The only time he saw an LP was in his grandparents' attic
CDs and diskettes are his parents' toys
What will his be?
Walkman   Discman   CD   MiniDisc   What's next?   SONY

" **Don't think new products or services. Think hits! A pop-star doesn't release a new single just to release it, but to make it go to number one in the charts. **"

From cool, to hot, to hit A hit has its phases of development. At first, there are a few people who like it and have heard of it, then the mass market awakens and begins to take an interest in your product or service and finally it is a best seller. The internet has developed along these same lines. At the start, there was a group of pioneers who thought 'Cool, we'll develop websites and see what happens,' while the broad mass market kept its distance. Then the industrial establishment woke up and started to build intranets and home pages. After a while came the users, the normal people, and a mass market was created.

On the internet, we have gone from something that I would say was cool, then became hot and was transformed into a hit. These are the stages:

- cool
- hot
- hit.

Hits are a matter of timing. Someone who launches a service during the cool phase can't count on many customers, but *can* count on a small number of devoted users; for example, that was where the internet banks in Sweden found themselves in 1996. When the number of users started increasing and the internet became hot around 1998, more companies sprang up, and offering financial web services and stock brokerage became widespread. Then, in 2000, financial services on the internet became a real hit with a host of new web services such as funds, insurance and mortgages. During this time, the internet banks in Sweden became a real mass market with over two million online accounts.

During the cool phase, there are few users and usually not enough substance for profitability. But it is a phase where pioneers can learn from advanced customers and where the risks are relatively small. Those who invest in the cool phase need a lot of stamina and need to know that the investment is at an early stage. A company launching in a cool market has the chance to be first, but there is nothing to say that if you are first you're guaranteed success in later phases. Being first you have to invest heavily in order to retain the head start, while at the same time teaching those coming afterwards.

The hot phase is optimal for investments; this is the phase just before the market really takes off and where there is enough substance for the market to be of interest. Companies launching in the hot phase have good possibilities of quickly building both brand and customer base at a relatively low cost.

If the market for a business idea is already a hit, the risks for investment are low, but the barriers to entry are high since a number of companies have already established themselves on this attractive market. Typical established hit markets today on the web are books, computers, and CDs. You need a superior business idea if you are a new company in order to compete with the established hit-makers.

Each individual company and the company's services and products all go through these phases from cool to hit, which are often a consequence of how the outside world develops and how services and products are received in this world.

Different customers belong to different phases. Geoffrey Moore described the phenomenon in his books *Inside the Tornado* and *Crossing the Chasm*. Early adopters buy a product or use a new service because it is new and no one else has it. On the mass market, the opposite is true: consumers buy because everyone else buys. Following others' behavior is safe.

❝EARLY ADOPTERS BUY A PRODUCT OR USE A NEW SERVICE BECAUSE IT IS NEW AND NO ONE ELSE HAS IT. ON THE MASS MARKET, THE OPPOSITE IS TRUE: CONSUMERS BUY BECAUSE EVERYONE ELSE BUYS.❞

I like to describe the cool phase as being built on individualism, and the hit phase on collectivism. This affects the marketing to these different customers. When Fondex was launched the advertisement campaign had a rebellious undertone and was about revolution on the fund market. This was hardly a message to the masses since a very small proportion of the population considers itself to be internet rebels, but it was a good way of getting attention and attracting the early adopters, the cool ones. In our next campaign, we changed the tone completely and marketed ourselves as a safe, family service with many satisfied customers.

Symbols of change

Business history in the 20th century has been the story of the big companies. The 21st century will be about the few, but very, very big corporations and the many, many, small ones. Small companies have become masters of driving change – not only within their own organizations but in their market as a whole. Usually this dynamic starts with the small company as a symbol of change. There is a lot of power in symbols of the future, but more as an idea than in terms of substance.

The symbol of change, The Movement, stands for something new that forces the other players in the market (i.e. the Establishment) to follow. It's a process that involves a lot of enthusiasm on the side of the start-up and much angst and frustration from the older companies. Even though a tiny company in a huge market doesn't have any real impact, it is usually annoying for the older companies to have an outsider as the symbol of the future. The effect is that the bigger companies must try even harder, just to take back some lost ground.

Even though the consumers typically have no initial role in this (they are normally happy with things as they are), the market will gradually change as a whole, driven by creative tension between large and small companies. It changes from the bottom up, and back to the bottom again.

This is the way that the Establishment and the Movement, the old and the new, together create the dynamics which shape the future, the actual outcome.

Fondex was a start-up and a symbol of change in the Swedish mutual fund market and introduced a new distribution model based on the transparency of the internet. The banks, representing the old distribution paradigm with offices where they sold their own set of funds, obviously felt threatened by the little company that offered consumers a single place for comparing and buying all funds. The market was oligopolistic with four banks controlling around 85 percent of all distribution channels and funds sold. Large banks and insurance companies that control the mutual fund business is the situation in most western European countries, except the UK where independent financial advisors represent some 50 percent of the distribution channels.

At the soul of a bank is the concept of control. Now, the mutual funds market suddenly became more uncontrollable and open. The four big Swedish banks – SEB, Nordbanken, FöreningsSparbanken and Handelsbanken – panicked, even though they could not do much about the free trade on the internet.

The journey to become a re-starter
The banks had nothing against the internet when they were setting the agenda themselves. Ever since 1996, when SEB opened one of Sweden's first major internet banking services, the banks were hailed as champions of the new economy. Sweden and Finland are the countries with the world's largest number of online banking customers per capita.

In the media, the old banks stood out as true re-starters. But in reality, they were not. They had merely digitized their traditional office and put it on the web. That's not change. It was still classic banking business, locking in customers and locking out alternatives. The openness of the web didn't characterize the banks. To become a re-starter is not merely about starting a new venture, it's more about going through a social and mental process.

Then, finally, the banks slowly changed to become real re-starters, both in body and soul. The process followed what I think is quite a typical path. The first reaction towards Fondex and other independent distribution channels on the mutual fund market was to pretend that these new companies didn't exist.

The next step, when the distribution channels not only became symbols of change but also growing operations that sold large numbers of mutual funds, including those of the banks, was to fight the companies by not paying out any commissions for sold funds, and to hinder the business in various ways.

The third stage was the breakthrough. Now, the banks became willing to negotiate agreements with the independent marketplaces, first on their own terms, then on equal terms. They realized that they could not have a substantial trading volume outside their control and compliance. The Movement was finally becoming part of the Establishment.

The final stage in a bank's journey towards becoming a re-starter is when large financial institutions finally accept and promote the openness of the internet's culture that is its main characteristic, and identify it as an opportunity. And subsequently they open up their own systems to other companies and competing products, just as they are providing other systems with their products on the open market. The only way to compete in this landscape is by brand and performance, as in any efficient market. This is nothing to be idealistic about, but openness is a prerequisite to being competitive.

" THE TRUE FINANCIAL RE-STARTER REALIZES THAT NO ONE OWNS THE CUSTOMER "

The true financial re-starter realizes that no one owns the customer – the customers own themselves and their choices – and the only thing the supplier of financial products and services can do is to put itself at the customers' disposal in the best way. In autumn 2000, Swedish banks came closer to this goal and started to provide a wider range of external funds to their customers. But still they had not reached the final stage in openness – to offer every fund in the market in direct competition with their own, and to let the customer make the choice. But it will happen.

BUSINESS: PUMP UP THE VOLUME

Maybe the start-ups, the Movement, are needed to show the big companies, the Establishment, the way, and make things happen faster than they would otherwise. It is also true that the start-up in, say, the financial industry, might not have a bright future because sooner or later the big guys will adopt the new business model and make it their own.

Small vs big

Many aspiring entrepreneurs leave safe employment to start afresh, build their own company, kick-start new vehicles for change. The flow from the old companies to small start-ups is one of our time's great migrations. The other great movement is entrepreneurs returning to the corporation and when the big companies buy the small companies, to get the good people and their ideas back. And never before have so many new projects of change started in big companies as a response to the rapid developments outside the companies. One of the new economy's most important features is the dynamic between small and big companies.

The dynamics between small and large companies is nothing but frictionless. The start-ups usually end up in conflict with the established players who feel threatened or harassed by the new kids on the block. Still, the fact remains that the market is changing, and in any paradigm shift new companies and ideas emerge, and consumers are offered new services from both new and old companies. Both the re-starter and the start-up have a good chance in this arena.

Let's make a comparison between a start-up like Fondex and the big bank, and take a look at their respective strengths and weaknesses.

The traditional institution – the Establishment

- Strengths
  - ownership of physical distribution network
  - large and loyal customer base
  - resources for marketing and product development
  - strong and trusted brand.

- Weaknesses
  - size – inflexible and slow-moving organization
  - strategic dilemma – own e-business competes with own physical network
  - bad consumer reputation, usually caused by fees, charges and lousy service
  - not independent, promotes itself rather than its customers
  - large fixed costs, vulnerable to price competition.

The small internet start-up – the Movement

- Strengths
  - a new service with new benefits for the consumers
  - speed – can move fast and exploit opportunities
  - independent and objective – creates good will
  - start-up culture – can accomplish a lot with limited resources
  - PR and attention – the media like rebels.

- Weaknesses
  - starts from scratch
  - no brand
  - no customer base (and it takes time to attract customers)
  - small resources, usually a bag of venture capital, and no positive cash flow.

The conclusion of this analysis is that both players have pretty good odds for succeeding in the short term if the market is strong, anyway. Taking a longer perspective, nobody knows – it is a question about how fast the big company can change and the small one grow.

Both companies have their strengths and weaknesses and the most important lesson is to be aware of them. The big company that forms strategies based on what other big companies are doing only gets half way in its understanding of the changing market and its own standing in relationship to this change. In summary:

- Big and small companies have a lot to learn from each other. The challenge for the small one is to think big, and for the big one to think small. Entertainment giant Bertelsmann joining forces with the file-swapping rebels at Napster to sell music online is one of the best examples of how the Establishment can get together with the Movement and create new business.

- The biggest mistake an established company can do is not to learn from the start-ups. The most dangerous mistake the start-up can do is to underestimate the big company. It might be slow, but it's not necessarily wrong.

- The first questions for the big company in times of change are: What would we do if were not a big company? What would we do if we didn't have thousands of employees and vast resources? What would we do if we were small and could do anything we wanted?

- For the established corporation, it can be a useful exercise to think: If we presented our business plan to an investor or venture capitalist, as a start-up, would they put their money into the company? Of course, if you are a listed company, the market makes this evaluation each day. But that is not the point. The point is to look at an old business with new eyes. To view your company as a start-up.

- For the small company, the question is reversed: How long can we keep up our advantage before the big company catches up, new start-ups enter the market, and the whole thing restructures? The small company must take the perspective of the big company.

CHAPTER EIGHT

Customers: The new community

WE ARE THE TRUE CONTENT OF OUR MEDIA.

MARSHALL MCLUHAN, MEDIA THINKER

Media is community What does the future look like? Think chat! In October 1999, the first version of the fantasy world Dobedo, where you are a fantasy figure chatting with other fantasy figures, was launched. The environment is fictive, but the communication is real.

At the beginning of 2000, Dobedo had 300,000 members in Sweden, and the newly started Dobedo in England had 125,000 members. And they had just launched in Germany … One day when I tried Dobedo and was chatting as my fantasy figure, someone wrote to me: 'Come on, let's go to the UK!' We did and continued chatting with the English. That is when I realized that Dobedo is the MTV of the future. Here is something that television can never achieve, and Dobedo's vision was to become the media company of the future.

Dobedo provides users with tools and environments, then the inhabitants of the fantasy provide the content and the entertainment. Value is created together.

the users = the company

No one knows beforehand what the result will be. When I spoke to one of Dobedo's founders, Rickard Kylberg, he asked himself: 'What will Dobedo look like in India?'

Think chat! Think global chat. Think parallel worlds that mean more than the real world because they are more real. Dobedo's future revenues come from real advertising and shopping that is integrated into the fantasy world. It is surely a model that yet has to be established. But the value to the user is clear, and it is not surprising that Sony invested in Dobedo. An interactive media channel aimed at the youth culture is what everyone is looking for.

Why do we consume the media? We are consuming entertainment. We are consuming facts and information. We are buying impressions and insights. But we also have a need for communication and community.

Media is about community. When Sweden played Brazil in the 1958 finals of the football world championship, many Swedes went out and bought a TV so that they could follow the match on television. It was the first big television happening in Sweden and television viewing took off from there.

That more and more people bought televisions in the 1960s was very much thanks to a man by the name of Lennart Hyland, a legendary Swedish TV personality. Those who did not follow Hyland's show were out in the cold. What created television in Sweden was not technology, but peer pressure. Inviting your neighbors over to watch television was a common occurrence, and if you didn't have a television could not invite the neighbors back. This quickly led to pressure on all the televisionless households to get 'connected.' Think 'Hyland' when you think media. Create a community that users want to be part of.

This is something that restaurants have learned: people attract people and then you have a positive spiral. Who wants to go into an empty restaurant? You want a nightclub that is heaving, so who wants a nightclub without a queue? This is something that the best websites have learned: users on the internet also want to be at busy places (as long as the servers are not jammed).

A community, or virtual community as it has been called, is a group of people with shared interests or values on the net. I can't see why this is less real than an association outside the net. Isn't speaking on the telephone just as real a form of communication as chatting at a café over lunch?

A community can be an expression for a group that likes the same thing. But that's a superficial way of looking at it. A sense of community is often defined more by what you don't like. Protests against nuclear weapons can quickly generate tens of thousands of signatures on the internet, and the Foundation against Nordbanken (a Swedish bank) was a heavily trafficked website for dissatisfied customers. That is more or less what a war is founded on: you fight what you don't like.

Many new web services are built on a common dislike. If you don't like insurance brokers, go to the unbiased marketplace for insurance on the web and make your own choice. If you don't like your bank, choose the new independent internet bank. If you don't like the price of CDs in the shops, go to Amazon.com. Community often sounds like a cozy gathering in cyber space. It isn't. Community on the net can be an unpleasant experience for companies who have something to hide.

> " SUCCESSFUL WEB COMPANIES MANAGE TO CREATE A COMMUNITY AROUND THEIR SERVICES. IT STARTS WITH YOU REPRESENTING SOMETHING THAT OTHERS WANT TO BE PART OF "

" Successful web companies manage to create a community around their services. This can be done in many ways, but it starts with you representing something that others want to be part of, rather like a political party (Dobedo's vision was to create the Dobedo Nation). "

From individual to collective

After a long period of pronounced individualism as a consequence of increasing liberalism in the 1980s, the collective has made a comeback. But the collective is no longer an expression for what everyone does together, as in the 1970s, but what some people do together.

During lunch with Jonas Bonnier, head of a division within the Bonnier Media Group, I realized something that I had not fully understood until then. How the conversation came about, I do not know, but it was natural that we were talking media since he was the new CEO at Bonnier Weekly Magazines and I was working at Icon Medialab, who had just delivered an intranet to the companies in the Bonnier sphere. Our conclusions helped me understand consumer markets better:

Wrong: me = me

Right: me = us

The opposite to me is not you. The opposite to me is them. The identification is to belong to a group.

You look for groups, for example, by joining a motorbike club, and you find out which groups you belong to, for example, by looking at the list of participants at a conference. A men's club, a hockey team or a jeans brand works the same way. They identify groups rather than individuals. The gang is the main thing. Content that answers the question 'Who am I?' is good content.

We are constantly looking for references to our environment, references that define who we are. 'You' is not about creating a unique solution that fits you and no one else. It's about you belonging to an environment that is bigger than you and where you fit in. You read an article in *FastCompany*, which others also read. You are part of the circle of readers, and this defines you. Here are some other examples:

- You receive an e-mail, and it's just as interesting to see who else is on the mailing list as it is to read the content. The address list defines who you are.
- You find a book at Amazon and immediately find out which other books you could buy – based on what others with the same taste have bought. You automatically belong to a group.

- You are a guest at a wedding, and read the guest list. You find out who else is there, which defines you and the group you are a part of.

Therefore I might also want to know:

- Who is watching the television program that I am watching right now?
- Who has read the book that I am reading right now?
- Who else is on this website right now?
- Who is like me?

In 1999 came Gooey. This was a piece of software from Israel, otherwise known for its unsuccessful peace processes, but famous among grateful surfers across the world for making the best applications for communication on the internet.

Free internet telephony came from Israel and ICQ (I seek you, a method for finding your friends on the internet) came from Israel. Gooey makes it possible to see who else is on the page you are on, if they also have Gooey, and to start talking. I logged into CNN and checked who else was reading an article about Clinton and started talking to a woman from Washington about the article. She had plenty to say. This book is not about all the cool things you can do on the internet, but about how it can be used to create value for an internet company.

At Fondex, there was a function that made it possible for users to send news articles to each other with a comment attached. This was very popular, and I was always surprised by the amount of information that flowed between our users, outside our control. We did not read the comments, but could see the volumes. We had created a benefit for our users, which would make them want to use our service, which in turn created value for the company.

There are probably many more people who would consider joining an existing group rather than starting up their own. You have to lower entry barriers to people who want to get involved. People, like myself, are lazy and we want services that help us to be lazy. And web customers are not only lazy. They are also the world's most rational customers. They want value, now, easily. Because they know they can get it.

It would probably be possible for a dissatisfied banking customer to gather some tens of thousands other dissatisfied customers with the help of the internet and then start a new bank. But this is only really a fun thing to say at conferences. No one can *really* be bothered to do this, but probably if we wait long enough, someone will probably ask us to join them as customers in their new bank.

When consumer markets such as telephony and energy are deregulated, we suddenly have many new alternatives to choose from. But we can't be bothered to do this on our own, so we go to services that help us make these choices. Just tell us who you are and we will make the choice for you.

In December 1997, I spoke at a conference arranged by the leading Swedish daily *Dagens Nyheter* (*DN*) for its advertisers. The point of the conference was to show the strength of a daily newspaper in spite of everyone talking about electronic media. And yes, there *is* strength in an established newspaper, and sure, electronic media have a lot to learn from the newspaper and how it works.

The first strength lies in the brand, which works like a quality platform in a world of increasing information chaos. But it may not matter whether the *DN* brand is distributed on paper, via the web or with smoke signals in the sky. That is why CNN is almost as big on the web as it is on television.

The second strength is the market share expressed in time for media consumption, where a majority of all Swedes read a morning paper and where this majority instinctively thinks that the newspaper is the main source of information. It's still top in people's mind.

The third strength is the interactivity, where readers actively participate with their own views and letters to the editor. The readers are a part of the content of the paper.

However, the greatest strength lies in the frame of reference. To be a *DN* reader means to belong to a group, and if you want to discuss the morning's news you would rather do it with someone who reads the same paper, and has read the same article. And the more people read the same paper, the more people you can communicate with, and the value of the group increases.

You have your own individual reading experience, but there is also a collective potential that increases the value. And for an advertiser, access to a strong group increases the value. In the network economy, you market yourself to the group, not the individual. That is why I don't agree entirely with the concept of one-to-one marketing.

A sense of belonging is to feel loyalty to something larger than yourself. Belonging creates trust, and this is something that a web company can never get enough of.

> **"A SENSE OF BELONGING IS TO FEEL LOYALTY TO SOMETHING LARGER THAN YOURSELF. BELONGING CREATES TRUST, AND THIS IS SOMETHING THAT A WEB COMPANY CAN NEVER ENOUGH OF"**

On January 10 2000 the world's largest merger was announced. AOL merged with Time Warner. In reality, it meant that AOL bought Time Warner with its own shares. AOL was a global internet service with approximately 22 million registered users, at the time of the deal. Time Warner encompassed, among other companies, the global television channel CNN which had millions of viewers across the world. Time Warner also had 120 million newspaper subscribers and 13 million cable-television households. If you only counted users and customers, Time Warner would be worth much more than AOL on paper.

But that is not the case. And the whole difference lies in the fact that AOL has linked its users to each other, while Time Warner sends its content mostly to passive, non-interactive and non-connected customers. That is web. That is network economy.

66 Network economy sounds very technical, rather like the square word 'broadband.' The networks that are linked together are in actual fact mostly people. If you are best at linking users and creating positive interactions you will become e-world champion. 99

Customers out of control
Napster is the world's largest file-sharing music community, a so-called peer-to-peer (P2P) service that lets users download files from each other's computers. This is how Napster works: You got to Napster's homepage to download the Napster application and then you can easily search and download music files from the computers in the community. Napster's software also provides members with a forum to communicate with one another via instant messaging and chat rooms. Anybody in the community can save music from their favourite CDs on mp3 files on their own hard disk and make files available for download, free of charge.

Shawn Fanning, Napster's founder, developed the original application in January 1999 while at Northeastern University, and then dropped out to start the company in May 1999. It was not long before the Recording Industry Association of America (RIAA) sued Napster for copyright infringement, in December 1999. About half a year later, in summer 2000, Napster had over 20 million users. In July 2000 a US court decided that the music-swapping company had to close. Well, Napster did not and the result was that both the company and Fanning turned into major media stars and the traffic on the website skyrocketed. The legal battle over Napster continued until March 2001, when a court finally ruled that Napster had to start blocking copyright protected songs from its service. Napster offered to voluntarily screen out titles that had been identified as copyrighted by record companies and artists. The filtering was not entirely successful and the first thing Napster members did was to find ways to get round restrictions. Napster had by then some 64 million users worldwide, an astonishing number. And the idea keeps on growing, even though several courts have established that file sharing of copyright protected music is illegal.

In October 2000, an unexpected move occurred in the middle of the battle. Media giant Bertelsmann seized the opportunity to become part of a movement and offered Napster an alliance to develop a subscription service. The alliance between Bertelsmann and Napster could prove even more significant than the famous old economy and new economy deal between Time Warner and AOL at the beginning of 2000. The big music corporations Vivendi Universal and Sony followed and announced their own move on the market for music downloads. Then in May 2001, Vivendi bought the music portal mp3.com. The website Duet Freenet is another P2P service that pools the power of member computers around the world, creating a virtual information store open to anyone to freely publish information of any kind. Of course, they take no responsibility for copyrights and it is also hard to find anybody to sue. Groove Networks, a company founded in October 1997, is yet another P2P initiative. Groove is internet communications software that allows people with shared interests to make direct connections for real-time interaction. With the Groove application, you can work, play or just hang out with the people. If you are a business, Groove offers a platform for managing projects, sharing documents, keeping a calender, having discussions and interacting with partners and customers.

What makes services like Napster, Freenet and Groove so valuable to the users is that they are all leveraging previously unused resources, by connecting the hundreds of millions of devices which have been connected to the internet. These services are also under the users' control, securely on the PC. The information passes outside the centrally controlled websites or servers. P2P operates at 'the edge' of the internet. The user chooses how to communicate, what to share and with whom. The paradigm of the P2P revolution is that it lies beyond control. It is outside the center. It is probably many companies' worst nightmare. The record industry versus Napster is one of the most vivid examples of the clash between the Establishment and the Movement. It also shows how hard it is to stop an idea that is right. File sharing between computers that allows users to download music for free simply offers irresistible user value, which is why a number of Napster clones have emerged like Gnutella, Opennap, Gnapter, Aimster, Knapster. And the music industry will continue changing. Napster and its fellow companies are wrongdoers in the eyes of the law, but the sheer volume of Napster's millions of members proves that the service has great user value. For the user it is the right thing, something that many other internet ventures have failed to offer. The main question for Napster and its partner Bertelsmann is how to transform the free service – which attracted so many users – into a paid subscription model. The internet has no problem providing great value for its users, like e-mail or file swapping, but the challenge for businesses is how to turn that value into cash flow and users into real customers. The golden rule remains: you have to find the value before you get the customers.

CHAPTER NINE

Communication: Tell your story

ALL EDUCATION SPRINGS FROM

IMAGES OF THE FUTURE

ALVIN TOFFLER, FUTURIST

9

Tell your idea – sell your idea

It doesn't matter how much you believe in your idea, as long as you're the only one to believe in it, you will be considered a day dreamer. Starting and running new businesses as well as changing established businesses is about making your ideas belong to others. You are an idea salesman. This is actually one of the key activities in a start-up or a re-start. Telling your story to others and getting them to believe it – as much as you yourself believe it. The recipients of your idea are many and varied, all of whom will have a significant part to play in your company:

- owners
- board of directors
- management
- employees
- investors
- media
- customers
- partners

First of all you have to sell the idea, then they might listen to the rest of what you have to say. And the ideas that you have to sell are not only the big vision, but also later, when you are running your company: each day you have to sell every idea that forms the company, everything from yearly budgets to which typeface should be used on the website.

We live in an ever more descriptive economy built on communicating ideas. If you want to start a company, you have to start by formulating the idea so that others will understand it. When Steven Spielberg was trying to sell one of his film ideas, he described the idea as follows: white killer shark attacks beach. The film company was hooked immediately and *Jaws* became a success. You're professional in everything else, aren't you? Become a professional storyteller too.

The need for storytellers is even greater for large companies faced with new challenges that demand change. In large companies, there is always an official future and a myriad of individual futures. Large companies are often a battlefield for different stories. The best storyteller wins. To be part of the Movement, you have to be able to communicate the Movement.

Leadership is about telling the way

What unites great leaders? During the 20th century, in times of turbulent change large fortunes were created through redistribution from the old to the new. The breakthrough of crude oil as a source of energy, and the growth of the car as a means of personal transport. The breakthroughs of film, radio then television. The first and second world wars. The computer as a personal tool. The internet. In every system shift, fortunes and opportunities are created for those who can make use of these changes, such as Henry Ford (Ford Motor Company), Sam Walton (Wal-Mart), Ingvar Kamprad (IKEA), and William Gates (Microsoft), to name but a few.

Apart from the fact that empires are built in times of system shifts, there are another three factors that unite great empire builders:

- They make products that improve the lives of the masses, rather than the few and the rich.
- They have the ability to see and understand the future, and to act on it. It is not always the innovator that is rewarded, but often the one who carries it out.
- They are driven by a solid vision.

A leader who can't describe where they are going is not a leader. Leadership is to a large extent about deciding the direction and taking others there with you. It often strikes me how few leaders and politicians today have a story about the future. I often get the feeling that the old leaders had a clearer picture of where they were going:

Moses and Ulysses – To get home

Karl XII – To get away from home

The French Revolution – Liberty, equality, fraternity

Theodore Roosevelt – The New Deal

But many of the new leaders have a picture of the future too:

Cisco – One planet, one network

Malaysia – The multimedia corridor

Nokia – Connecting people

Credit to the person with the right story. Look at Skandia. Few can tell you the name of the CEO of this global insurance and asset management company. On the other hand, many have heard of Leif Edvinsson who pioneered the study of intellectual capital. When he worked for Skandia he wasn't even part of Skandia's group executive board but was nevertheless probably the best-known person in the whole company. Why? Because he has a compelling story to tell about intellectual capital.

He headed the redefinition of Skandia from an insurance company to an innovation company, and he created the symbolic Skandia Future Center out in
Waxholm, in the archipelago outside Stockholm, where other world leaders
would be invited to come and discuss the future. There, you can relax in a
comfortable armchair, look out on the archipelago, smell the aroma of tar and
newly baked cakes, with soft music playing in the background. Right opposite
sits the guru of intellectual capital, Leif Edvinsson and explains that it's about
brain-stilling, not brain-storming. Then he asks you: 'What does the future
smell like?' Wow.

It is obvious that it is more interesting spending time at a Future Center with
Leif than it is at headquarters in Stockholm.

Before you invest in any shares, find out if the group CEO surfs on the internet.
In large companies, it is always the case that you look to the group CEO for
guidance in prioritizing. The group CEO sets the agenda for the group management team, which in turn sets the agenda for the middle management, who in
turn affect the rest of the employees in the company. Therefore the top position
in a company has an almost creepy influence on the culture in the company.
You are rewarded for agreeing and keeping in line. If group CEOs dismiss the
internet, as many CEOs did in the mid-1990s, the internet ends up at the
bottom of the list of priorities. If they are positive towards the internet, the
whole company is positive to the internet. Companies mean extreme hierarchies, for better or worse. If the top is bad, the whole company becomes bad.

A company leader's attitude is at least as important as their official story of the
future. A couple of years ago, the financial paper *Dagens Industri* interviewed
company leaders about their internet habits. What surprised me the most was
that Håkan Mogren, then CEO at Astra (which was later merged to become
Astra Zeneca), boasted about the fact that his secretary printed his e-mails on
paper for him, while Leif Johansson, group CEO at Volvo said that he spent
one hour per day surfing the web. I don't think a person in Leif Johansson's

position has time to surf one hour per day. The important thing is that he said he did. He wanted to communicate an attitude.

I believe that large companies have a lot to gain from thinking web and from developing new digital services. This is perhaps not a completely unconventional attitude today. In an insurance company, for example, with millions of customers, customer handling is one of the largest costs. Interactive customer solutions via the internet can make customer interactions more efficient and could, long term, lower costs by say, 20 to 30 percent each year, which is directly reflected in the profits (or in the form of freed up resources that can be invested into increasing competitiveness). Which in turn will be reflected in the share price. If the group management has a hesitant attitude to the internet, I would never buy shares in that company as I don't believe that they can be competitive in the long run.

Equity analysts across the world, who, to a large extent, form the market's valuation of listed companies should, in my opinion, look closer at the boss's attitudes instead of analyzing the balance sheet. Interview the company leaders about their willingness to invest in the future, and about their own habits. Are they connected? If not: Sell!

In early 2001, telecom giant Ericsson ran into problems and their share fell rapidly. On stage at press conferences, at the center of the drama was the hunted CEO, Kurt Hellström, who repeatedly failed to communicate Ericsson's future.

> **EQUITY ANALYSTS ACROSS THE WORLD SHOULD LOOK CLOSER AT THE BOSS'S ATTITUDES INSTEAD OF ANALYZING THE BALANCE SHEET**

Presentation techniques – back to basics

When you are trying to convey an idea, good presentation technique helps. The best presentation technique, but also the hardest, is the spoken word. Standing on a stage and telling a story.

When I have been developing my presentations, it was mostly about technology. I started with the spoken word, experimented quite a bit with technology, and now I'm back at the spoken word.

> **"** THIS ABILITY
> TO PRODUCE AN
> INANE NUMBER
> OF OVERHEADS
> HAS BECOME
> THE
> CARICATURE OF
> A MANAGEMENT
> CONSULTANT **"**

When I was a child I used to tell jokes. I probably only knew one or two jokes, which I told over and over again, and they probably weren't even funny. But I presume that I got the right response that children get, and I developed a certain confidence and belief in the spoken word. At school I learned to use overheads, transparent film that you can write bullet points on. Much later, as a management consultant, my colleagues and I produced an innumerable number of overheads when we presented models, ideas, and conclusions to various clients. This ability to produce an inane number of overheads has, I guess, become the caricature of a management consultant.

Personally, I had an unshakeable faith in overheads. This faith was broken in 1994 when I was hosting the Multimedia Day, an international conference about new media that I co-organized. I opened the conference with the help of – an overhead. Many people reacted strongly to this and asked me why I didn't live and learn and use multimedia instead. I didn't have a good answer and was forced to admit that I was a victim of routine.

After this, I started to experiment with computer presentations. In the mid-1990s, the technology was regrettably not particularly developed and it was always as embarrassing for me or anyone else who attended a conference to speak about technology when one's own technology never worked. There were so many different cables and plugs, and half the time the PC didn't comply with the projector. Today, it's hardly ever the technology that fails.

So I stopped using computers and went over to slide shows. This was a result of the fact that I had reduced the textual content in my presentations and instead used more images, such as adverts, photographs, and other symbols. Apart from the fact that the computer did not always work, the large number of images (I could use over one hundred images in a 30-minute presentation) meant that the memory capacity of the hard drive was insufficient. Slides are an old, dependable technology that seldom cause problems and deliver perfect, photo-like image quality. Many conference organizers thought I was joking when I told them that I was going to use slides – they hadn't heard of this since their school days. But it worked. Then something happened that made me stop using anything that could be called a visual aid. I realized that the best speakers did not have any assistance at all.

I started taking drama lessons from a theater director. And I am convinced that my one term with Shakespeare taught me more than my four years at Stockholm School of Economics, not just with regard to management, but also communication. Hamlet can be more valuable than an MBA. Managing a company has similarities to a theatre. The director is the decision-maker in the play, but everyone is part of it. The boss should not be administrator, but inspirator.

There is a wonderful image of leadership on the cover of a Swedish monthly magazine, *Månadsjournalen*. It shows director Ingmar Bergman and the actors in the production of a new play. The group picture is in the form of an upside-down pyramid, with the 80-year-old Ingmar Bergman alone on the floor, at the bottom, at the front in a pair of Nike sneakers. The actors stand behind him. The whole ensemble is needed for the play, but there is no question who is the boss, and the director's role is so obvious that he can just as well be on the floor. But to mark the mutual dependency, Ingmar Bergman has his hand firmly gripped in Elin Klinga's, the leading actress.

When I started taking drama lessons, I realized that I should scrap all form of visual aid and concentrate on Shakespeare. What I learned from the theater with regard to presentation technique was how to get across to the audience the images that I myself saw. These images that come from within are always stronger than external images produced on overheads or slides. Theater, in the sense of the spoken word and the images that it creates, is multimedia. I am no Richard Burton, but I do my best.

Before you can start speaking, you need a stage. Just because you're standing on a stage, it doesn't mean that you have one. You must have the audience's complete attention before it is meaningful to start talking. Many speakers walk on to the stage, traipse about and speak too fast, and the audience, not knowing what to focus on, tires.

A speaker must be the focal point, and express the fact that 'Here I am and you are now going to listen to me.' One of the most dramatic things you can do on a stage is to just stand there and do nothing. Soon, after just a few seconds, the excitement increases in the room and the audience's eyes are turned towards the stage: what's happening? After this, you can say practically anything and, if you have a good introduction, you can keep the audience's attention for hours. When you are going to speak, practice standing on the stage in front of the audience for 10 seconds without saying a word. If you can handle this, you can handle anything.

The theater is an effective form of communication. It is based on communicating images and feelings. As a storyteller, you have to understand, see and feel yourself in order for the audience to understand.

Don't point at your overhead, visualize instead the images you have in your head and that you want your audience to see. It is a magical and powerful form of suggestion. 'See' what you are talking about. When I tell people that in two years, half of all cars sold will be via the internet, I see before me millions of households throwing themselves at their computers. The image is transmitted.

Be simple, like a rock song. Shakespeare is simple. Shakespeare is rock 'n' roll. Why? Because he writes about eternal, universal human problems, things that affect us all. It is elementary, but nevertheless extremely hard. Isn't pop the same? Love, jealousy, revenge, anguish. This is the most banal – and the hardest. You have to have respect for the simplest. You also have to like the simplest.

❝ SHAKE-SPEARE IS SIMPLE. SHAKESPEARE IS ROCK 'N' ROLL ❞

Shakespeare's plays have similarities to television's soap operas. The strength in soap operas lies in the audience following every word that is uttered. It's the same with theater; you mustn't lose the audience for a second.

Rhetoric is a large and interesting subject, but personally I think what really makes a good speaker stand out is their feel for what they are telling. Then there are many tricks for putting the words in the right order and for arguing your cause. But I think it has more to do with pedagogy. Richard Normann taught me to first teach a language, then speak it. Instead of saying 'The internet will change the world' (and half the audience is lost), explain first what the internet is – then explain how it will change the world. And you will change the world.

Finally, I would agree with a writer I know, who says: 'If you want to say something new, wear a tie.' It's better to look conservative when you are going to deliver radical changes.

PR – a part of the day-to-day business

I have learned that the best way to handle public relations is to treat the media and journalists as normal people. Many companies and business leaders are afraid of the media, and they are of course a powerful force which demands respect. But you must also realize that the media are part of reality for a company and you must develop good relationships with them. Just treat the media like you would treat anybody else; be polite and honest. And make contact.

Make your own media list

I never bother much with PR agencies. They charge too much for nothing. It's better to develop your own list of daily papers, magazines and publications – and the people to call. At Fondex we had a list of some 300 important journalists and every time we had a press release we just e-mailed it ourselves. There was never a need for a PR agency. It doesn't take very long to assemble such a list, just call the papers and ask for e-mail addresses.

❝I NEVER BOTHER MUCH WITH PR AGENCIES. THEY CHARGE TOO MUCH FOR NOTHING❞

Call journalists yourself

I often call journalists to communicate what's happening in the company, to release news exclusively, or just to have a friendly chat. I have many journalist friends, and I appreciate our conversations. Also, I think it is good to develop a natural relationship with the media. They, on their side, also appreciate getting news from the source. If the only news they ever get is a communiqué from a PR agency, they won't care much about the company in the long run. Or they will write about it as if it *were* a stranger.

Keep a low profiles

It can be a fantastic feeling when the press writes good things about you and your company and makes you the hero of the day. But you must also know that everything that goes up must come down. You can be certain that for every good article that is written about you, there will eventually be a bad one. And the better the good ones, the worse the bad ones when they come. It is almost a natural law of media. I have several friends who rose to fame in the web's early days and became legendary business leaders overnight in the super-hot new economy. Their faces were all over the business magazines. Then they got too much positive press and the media felt an urge to burst the bubble and kill their public image by harassing them and their companies when times got harder. Well, it has happened to me too. It's a tough game, and you have to be prepared to play it. In the long run, it's always better to keep a low profile. You have nothing to lose and everything to gain.

66 Make PR and external communication a part of the culture of your company. Just as with customer service, it is fatal to outsource PR. Have a dialog within the company about what you want the outside world to learn about you, and communicate it, preferably personally, to journalists. The media are not a monster, just treat it right. And always keep a low profile and never promise more than you can deliver. 99

To be optimistic

Why do negative people seem to be smarter, and positive people naïve? To criticize makes you look better, like you have thought it through. If you are optimistic, you risk appearing vulnerable. The new economy has a tendency to be very optimistic about everything, especially the demand for new technology.

Should you be optimistic or pessimistic? Should you have a happy-go-lucky view of the future or be cynical, negative and critical? My friend Ole hates optimists. He says there is nothing to be optimistic about and that being optimistic is a pretty useless attitude – to welcome change with an open heart without reservation. I understand him. It's rather like not thinking at all; it follows that thinking people, real thinkers, are always critical. Schopenhauer, the old pessimist, was once asked why he didn't commit suicide. The old man replied that that wouldn't solve anything; not even his suicide change would lead to anything better. And he was right in a sense.

In 1996, there was a large exhibition at the Museum of Modern Art in Stockholm. Young artists exhibited works under the theme 'About time.' It was about time, our time. The piece of art that captured me, at an otherwise fairly dull exhibition, was a 1-metre cube, made of pure, black asphalt. I was there at the opening, and the cube was perfect with sharp edges. Asphalt, however, has the property of slowly melting, losing its shape, with time; it is a fluid, but very thick and viscous. When I returned, a couple of months later, the asphalt cube had sunken into a black lump on the floor. It was horrible and brilliant. Was that how the young artist saw the time he was living in, as a thick, sinking goo? When the daily paper *Expressen* reviewed the exhibition, they thought it was depressing. The same type of exhibition during the 1960s would have been seen to be a provocative optimism. I like this expression – provocative optimism for the future. That is what the internet industry stood for at the beginning.

> **"** IT IS NO LONGER UNUSUAL FOR A NEWLY STARTED COMPANY TO HAVE PLANS TO BECOME GLOBAL NUMBER ONE AT ONCE. NOTHING IS IMPOSSIBLE **"**

Optimism is provocative. It is irrational, senseless and uncritical in a time when a lot is rational and well grounded. When the establishment says: 'The guy refuses to accept facts,' I know that it is someone who could be on the right track. It is no longer unusual for a newly started company to have plans to become global number one at once. Nothing is impossible – I like that mentality.

Spokesmen for the Movement have delivered vision after vision, one more fantastic than the other. At the same time, the Establishment have called the internet industry not serious. They have been provoked by the optimism. They have said that is doesn't work, it is impossible, it will not last.

During autumn 1999 and early 2000, discussions of the so-called internet bubble were well under way, both in the US and Europe. It seemed as though those within the industry could not see a bubble (or at least said it would be hard to burst), while those outside were warning that the bursting of the bubble was imminent. This disagreement can be a sign that those within were blinkered and those outside were unable to understand. Then there were powerful people from within the industry who began to speak aloud of the valuations being too high, such as Microsoft's Steve Ballmer. Then, a signifi-cant number of external analysts came out and professed that the whole internet industry was way too undervalued and that it was time to invest even more heavily in Nasdaq – it would only get more expensive with time. However, finally the critics won and the internet bubble burst in the autumn of 2000.

You must make the decision yourself whether you are an optimist or not. If I am the only representative for my industry at a dinner party, I feel it's my duty to defend it in discussions. If I am among colleagues, I criticize it. If you represent a company in a crazy industry, be prepared for constant confronta-tions. You decide what stance you take.

If you are a company leader and an entrepreneur, there is one thing you have to realize. You are leading a company, whose earnings are expected in the future and whose analysts and shareholders have invested their money on your ability to create growth. They have, in other words, invested in your positive belief in the future. That is actually the main asset they have invested in. I wouldn't say that they have invested in a totally uncritical future optimism, but if you were to express yourself pessimistically about the future, it would be the same as if a Formula One driver, who had just signed a multi-million dollar contract, said that he didn't like speed. You would wonder what you had just invested in.

66 Optimism sounds like gullibility, rather like hoping everything will turn out all right, irrespective of what the figures say. Pessimism, on the other hand, is based on the view that everything will be disastrous. Both are actually quite bad. The main thing is that you believe in what you do. That belief, if it is honest, can never be criticized. 99

Clichés, new words, and the lack of words

Times of rapid change create a need for new words, words that can express what is happening. We all have a chance to find definitions for what is happening. To create the future, by building companies, is just as much about describing it, with new words and expressions. It is a form of experimentation that also leads to our time's clichés.

We have never been part of so many revolutions as right now: the information technology revolution, the internet revolution, the knowledge revolution, the

66 REVOLUTION IS A STRONG WORD THAT USED TO MEAN A VIOLENT POLITICAL UPHEAVAL, BUT NOWADAYS IT CAN JUST AS EASILY REFER TO THE LAUNCH OF A NEW PC MODEL 99

wireless revolution, and so on. Revolution is a strong word that used to mean a violent political upheaval, but nowadays it can just as easily refer to the launch of a new PC model. Watch out for revolutions.

When no one can explain what is happening, we say that there is a new economy separating itself from the old economy. But those who run businesses know that the economy – the allocation of scarce resources – hasn't changed much. However, companies' and consumers' behavior have probably changed to a certain degree. 'The old world' and 'the new world' are spoken of. We actually live in the world and it is made up of that which is new and that which is old. Find out what is really new.

The words that we do have are kneaded, exhausted, and stretched in both desperation and enthusiasm in order to convey what is happening around us in a new world. Words such as 'competence' are given a renaissance and are used to express everything from a company's services to authorities' qualifications and individual people's curriculum vitae. 'Network' can mean infrastructure, discussion forum or organizational chart. And the famous 'e-' is used as a prefix for anything that wants to appear modern.

There is a lack of nuances. Something is obviously happening around us, but we can't communicate it. Compare that to something such as alcoholic intoxication which has a rich language full of nuances and exact expressions. Similarly, when it comes to the two factors that are cornerstones in the industrial era – work and capital – there is a long tradition and a broad flora of words which describe what we mean, from consulting to manual labor (for work) and long-term investments to speculation (for capital).

New jobs lead to new words. When jobs change, we lack words. And the meaning of 'unemployed' has become totally misrepresentative, since many formally unemployed people work and many who formally work do not have a fixed contract but are instead 'free agents.'

The fact that we are using well-known words such as 'knowledge' to describe everything and anything is not so strange. The new is by definition hard to put a name to, and the words we have are used as best as possible. There is always a link from the old to the new.

The future is expressed with the help of the past, the already known. When the car came, it was called the 'horseless carriage' in the US. As time went by, we learned that it was in actual fact a whole new power, which would among other things make the development of suburbs and shopping centers possible. The television was called 'radio with pictures' at first, but unlike radio, television divided values and created the youth culture, rock 'n' roll.

In the beginning of the 1990s, we invented the expression 'information highway,' a motorway where loads of information rushes by. Now we are beginning to realize that it is something else, a dissolution of time and place with a new sort of information and without the distance that a motorway implies.

In the same way, we say 'knowledge society' and mean a society that is similar to the society of today but full of knowledge and where everyone is more educated. But more and more are beginning to realize that it is also something else. A society divided by new lifestyles and digitization, an explosion of ideas where the parts are falling into place in constant new patterns. But what is happening is expressed with old and frayed phrases that no longer mean anything.

If you don't formulate your own ideas of the future, someone else will. And the competition is fierce. 'Connecting people' says Nokia; 'Just do it' says Nike; and 'Where do you want to go today?' says Microsoft. You decide. You choose which stories you want to listen to. And what stories you want to tell. You create the Movement.

CHAPTER TEN

Failures: The Encyclopedia of Mistakes

FAILURE IS LACK OF SUCCESS.

COLLINS COBUILD, ENGLISH LANGUAGE DICTIONARY

The Encyclopedia of Mistakes

I fail often and in many different ways. To use a cliché: I could fill a whole book on failing. Imagine a large, black leather-bound dictionary: The Encyclopedia of Mistakes – a systematic run-through of the nature of defeat. There are so many different sorts of mistakes: small, big, acceptable, unacceptable, instructive, unnecessary, one-offs. Blessing-in-disguise mistakes, all's-well-that-ends-well mistakes, wrong-decision-at-the-last-minute mistakes, devastating mistakes, unnoticeable mistakes, mistakes with immediate effect, mistakes that are discovered long after the event. There are small mistakes, like getting the day wrong for a meeting. There are huge mistakes, such as trying to seize Moscow during the winter (not my mistake). Everyone can make a mistake. Making the right mistakes is an art.

A while ago, I met some people at a company and we started talking about leadership. Someone asked me what advice I used to give new employees. In order to keep the list short, I chose one piece of advice: 'Dare to make mistakes.' The attendant question was quick: 'Do companies really accept mistakes?' It is a good question. Can companies really accept mistakes, or is this something that they just say?

The knowledge society is not a place where anything goes. If someone asked me, I would answer that you can definitely not accept all mistakes. In my opinion, mistakes made in an area where there is existing competence are unacceptable. Mistakes can be avoided by recruiting competent people who have the required competence. A person recruited for the post of CFO is expected to master accounting. A CFO who makes mistakes in tax legislation is incompetent.

Since we run companies where there is not always the knowledge we need, we have to experiment. Mistakes are acceptable – a way of seeking knowledge – in areas where there is no ready competence.

Making mistakes is all right, but repeating the same mistake is inexcusable. Whoever makes the same mistake over and over again has not learned anything and does not belong in a knowledge company.

The knowledge society is both hard and soft at the same time. This gives us the chance to do what we have always done to get ahead, testing and learning. But the caveman who time and time again tries to make a fire using wet sticks will not survive. The challenge is both humanistic and Darwinistic. Be a human, play, and think. Be a human, live, and survive. A company has to build a culture around the nature of failure.

To minimize the cost of failure

Golf is a perfect combination of structure and chaos. The structure in golf is rock hard: 18 holes, 14 clubs, one ball, and a book of rules issued by Royal St Andrews in Scotland. Not to mention the unwritten laws that govern behavior and dress code on the course. But it doesn't matter how much you practice. No perfect structured golf swing in the world can compensate for the chaos that characterizes the game. No one knows how the ball will bounce when it hits the ground, no one knows if your partner will lose control and throw his bag into the water and go home, no one knows how the weather will turn out after four hours on the course, no one knows how the ball that went into the woods lies until you find it and have to use all manner of creativity to hit a decent shot from behind a tree stump. It is chaotic. Totally unpredictable. Yet predictable.

The strange thing is that the same company leader, who in his organization strives to minimize risk, chaos and uncomfortable surprises, happily swings his driver right across a wooded area just to see whether he can reach the green in one shot. Why? Because if it's possible to test an idea, for many it's irresistible to try and find out whether it holds.

This driving force needs to be recognized. In 90 percent of cases, you fail, but in the other 10 percent, you have a success. The barrier is tested. The ball landed on the green. It was possible to carry it off.

The reason why many are ready to take risks on the golf course, even if losing is painful, is that the cost of failure is comparatively small for most players. In companies, the cost of failure is enormous. Not only in economical terms, but also from a personal perspective: if you fail you're cast aside. That is not the case on the golf course. Bad shots can happen to anyone.

“As a company leader, you have a responsibility to minimize the cost of failure, both economically and personally, but at the same time to create an environment that encourages new ideas and entrepreneurial spirit, risk-taking, and experimentation. This is done by making projects small, simple, and cheap. Then the decision to start is not so hard, and the fall – if it occurs – is not so hard. ”

Inverted success
There is nothing that says that all those companies operating at a loss today will become profitable in the future. But from a narrow perspective, many have fallen into the trap that I call 'inverted success' (sounds a bit like perverted success).

Many internet companies were world champions at attracting media attention and high valuations. But they didn't get any customers, or at least not enough customers. And the more attention they got, the higher were the expectations from the outside world: 'They must have a lot of customers, since they are so famous.' And it didn't really matter how many new customers the company got, how much revenues increased, or how successful the company was. It is always too small compared to expectations. Some increased their costs in proportion to increasing revenues and consequently made losses on each unit sold. You never caught up. The greater the success, the greater the failure. This is inverted success.

❝ IN COMPANIES, THE COST OF FAILURE IS ENORMOUS. NOT ONLY IN ECONOMICAL TERMS, BUT ALSO FROM A PERSONAL PERSPECTIVE: IF YOU FAIL YOU'RE CAST ASIDE ❞

Fondex was caught in this trap. The company received a lot of attention after the launch in May 1999. In a couple of months, there had been hundreds of articles in the daily and business press, both in Sweden and abroad. What everyone wanted to know, of course, was how many customers the company had. No figures were published, and I know that however many customers the company could show, it would never correspond to the enormous attention that Fondex had got in such a short time. The success in relation to actual results would immediately be seen as a failure, or an inverted success – something that is actually a great success, but looks like a failure.

A newly started company doesn't count on showing respectable revenues until after a couple of years, when the company has reached a considerable size. Therefore, receiving a lot of attention in the early stages is a risk – it makes the company seem as if it is big already. All progress gives the opposite effect and the company appears small and a failure.

Why companies fail

Companies fail, that's part of life. Apart from purely economical reasons such as money running out and companies going bankrupt, there is a long list of other reasons why companies fail. One of the most common reasons is probably that the challenge is underestimated. For example, the internet had a reputation for being a place where you could earn lots of money fast. This has been proved wrong.

The net is not easy. Being successful on the internet is probably the hardest thing on earth, which is supported by the fact that so few internet companies are actually earning any money. Here are some more reasons for why companies fail.

The management

What you didn't learn at business school is that everything comes down to people. If the management doesn't work, the company can sink quickly. A start-up or a re-start is about leadership and often a very special type of leadership, namely to project-manage an idea from vision to reality. The people in the managerial body need to support each other, all the time. The management must never fall apart, and if it does, it must be repaired immediately. Look after your management team, they are your best friends. Never desert them and make sure they never desert you. This is your gang, and those who are working with you are doing so because they believe in your idea.

The most important success factor in every company is good people working well together. What often goes wrong is a lack of cooperation and people who can't fulfill their tasks. I am not blaming them; there are a thousand reasons why people can't fulfill what they should have done. They didn't have time, they weren't competent, they didn't care enough, they weren't motivated enough, they couldn't prioritize, and so on. I am not blaming them – I blame myself, being responsible for recruitment.

What makes me feel like a loser most is to be part of a losing team where I myself have chosen the team members. I have also failed many times to recruit the right people because I have been in too much of a hurry. I have failed to motivate others because I have been too busy with something else. I have fought for ideas that proved to be the wrong ones.

> " BEING SUCCESSFUL ON THE INTERNET IS PROBABLY THE HARDEST THING ON EARTH, WHICH IS SUPPORTED BY THE FACT THAT SO FEW INTERNET COMPANIES ARE ACTUALLY EARNING ANY MONEY "

Companies that start pulling in different directions can fail fast. There is a difference between having creative tension in the company and having destructive conflicts about the direction you are taking. When a company grows, more people come in with more ideas, and the company becomes a place with many wills. Companies without a shared vision risk failing.

The board

After the management team, an active and competent board of directors is an important prerequisite for a company to be successful. A board should be senior and in the best of cases form a counterbalance to the mad entrepreneurs running the company. But even sensible entrepreneurs need advice from people who have more experience. A good board is your best support as entrepreneur. You can learn a lot from more senior people who know things better than you. The most common mistakes have been made before and a board can recognize the traps.

First and foremost the board's job is to make decisions, and when a company is newly started, there are a vast number of decisions to be made in a short time frame. Therefore, it is important that the board is kept well informed.

> **66 ALL TOO OFTEN, BOARDS IN NEWLY STARTED COMPANIES ARE MADE UP OF PEOPLE WHO SIT ON SEVERAL OTHER BOARDS AND WHO MAY NOT ALWAYS HAVE THE TIME TO GET STUCK INTO THE DETAILS OF YOUR COMPANY 99**

A board in a start-up should meet at least once a month during the first year. Being wise is not enough, a board also has to be able to dedicate the time required to your company. All too often, boards in newly started companies are made up of people such as venture capitalists and entrepreneurs who sit on several other boards and who may not always have the time to get stuck into the details of your company. Give board members share options in your company and demand a commitment from them. You should demand at least 150 hours per year from your board members.

The board has a formal responsibility which is sometimes forgotten. Boards usually like strategic business planning and discussing new opportunities. However, there is a risk that practical problem-solving gets pushed aside. I have sent several letters to my board to report on liquidity problems and additional financing needs. It's not much fun, but as CEO, you are responsible for informing and engaging the board. At certain times I have failed to engage the board and the decisions taken have been sub-optimal as a result.

Technology

Many entrepreneurs think that a good business model is enough. At one time, it was said that a good business model was the only important thing, even for a high-tech company like a web business. I think this is rubbish. Nothing can help a company that doesn't have technology under control. Recruit the best programmers – and if you are using consultants, use the best even if they are the most expensive. You can never underestimate the importance of choosing the right supplier, as the switching costs are high. One mistake Fondex made in the beginning was that we didn't hire any programmers of our own, but bought everything externally from a supplier that was not good enough.

Many people think that 'a web agency can sort out the technology' and that the hard part is marketing the website, resulting in entrepreneurs budgeting a couple million dollars extra for marketing in the business plan. Use this money on getting the technology right instead.

The best way of controlling technical development is probably to have your own development team. When I met one of the founders of price-comparison website Pricerunner.com, he explained to me that one of their key success factors was the fact that they had their own technical team of programmers and developers. This meant that they could develop solutions faster, safer, and they also had many new unique ideas which helped them be competitive.

Greed

In companies whose value increases quickly, greed can just as quickly become a problem. One person starts in March and gets share options at one price, and another person starts in April and by then the company has already increased in value and those who start later are given options at a higher price. After a year, during which both have worked flat out, the person who started one month earlier is suddenly twice as rich. Or, if the company went bust, they're both equally poor.

A good piece of advice is to be open about options and values from the outset. In September 1999 I met the CEO of an internet company who jokingly suggested including the current value of the options in the job description. 'We are currently recruiting at a price of ...' It might not be such a bad idea! The CEO in question had just completed three share issues in the space of a couple of months and had seen the absurd effects the share options had had on the employees who had received them, while the company increased from zero in value to nearly 200 million dollars in just over six months. A couple of weeks' difference in the starting date of employment was suddenly worth a couple of million.

Of course, you also have the reverse effect when the same company might lose 90 percent of the value in the same time and the options become worthless.

> 66 MANY TRY TO SNATCH AS MUCH AS POSSIBLE, AND THE RESULT IS RUINED RELATIONSHIPS THAT CAN NEVER BE REPAIRED. PEOPLE SHOW THEIR TRUE SELVES WHEN MONEY IS ON THE TABLE 99

In a start-up, both entrepreneurs and venture capitalists often become greedy. The entrepreneur does not want to sell too much and the investors want as much as possible for a small price. I have learned not to be greedy in the beginning. If everyone acts out of self-interest, it will all amount to nothing, and that applies to all companies. You have to be generous. But I have also learned to be watchful, otherwise you end up with too little. When the company is eventually sold or made public, many try to snatch as much as possible, and the result is ruined relationships that can never be repaired. People show their true selves when money is on the table.

The structure

You can learn a lot from the rocket industry when you structure the ownership in a newly started company. A rocket that is misdirected by a couple of millimetres on the ground can be several miles off-course once it is up in space. When a company is newly started, 1 percent's ownership back or forth is of no great consequence, but once public this percentage point can mean a differ-ence of millions of dollars. Perceived injustice can bring a lot of indignation up to the surface.

The legal structure of a company is important, both with regard to ownership and rewards. A growing company immediately acquires several parties with a vested interest: subsidiary managers, employees, and investors. The degree of complexity increases. This can be seen when the company is sold, if not before, when everyone who has invested money, time or something else wants compensation and their share of the profit. A company must be pre-pared to be sold in order to fit into another structure. The former structure must be in order so that transparency exists and the company's ownership structure can easily be seen.

Successful companies who manage to avoid greed in the beginning might notice that it rears its ugly head later on. The best thing you can do is to have a good structure of shares to investors and options to employees from the outset. It is impossible to make it absolutely fair, but the main thing, as I see it, is that those who are going to do the job are satisfied: the founder/entrepreneur and the management team. The problem is that the investors are often more inter-ested in guarding their investment and so, instead of rewarding employees, they force them to sign strict employment contracts to further lock up the assets/people. The investors, on the other hand, probably think that the employees are too greedy.

The doers

A potential problem in larger, established companies is the conflict between employees and shareholders with respect to the options program. An options program means that an employee with options has the right to buy shares at a predetermined price in the future. If the share price is higher than the option's strike price, the employee makes a profit. The thought behind this is to motivate the employees to stay and build value for the company. The problem, from a shareholder's perspective, is that when new shares are given to employees, the shareholding is diluted. The more options that are given to employees, the more the existing shareholders' shares are diluted. There is here, in other words, a new form of conflict between capital and work. This conflict can lead to the employees, the doers, losing faith and leaving the company for somewhere where they can get more return for their work. A company where this happens has failed.

Create energy! Give the doers power! Anybody can make decisions about the broad direction, but it is the operative people who build the company and who create quality on a detailed level. You have to dedicate your soul to each and every detail to get it right. Reducing future rewards by distributing too few options, by controlling the doers through strict employment contracts or strict lock-ups are ways of reducing the energy. You have to support the doers.

The capital

A good way of avoiding problems later is to invest appropriately in the beginning of a new project. Find the balance. Too much money can make the entrepreneur and the employees wrongly focused, too little puts a brake on the business. The money must not run out. A start-up lives on venture capital until it achieves sufficient cash flow, and the only way to secure growth is to attract more venture capital. Straight after the first financing round you have to start planning the second. And when you have completed the second round, you have to start on the third. It is often easy to get venture capital for the first round when an investor sees the opportunity of acquiring 50 percent in a newly started company for a relatively small sum of money. Then the investors hope that someone else will come in and inject the big bucks into the next round.

A common problem is that too little is invested in the first round, which leads to the whole project suffering. Subsequent share offerings are made too early, and at each stage the entrepreneur becomes less and less motivated as their ownership is diluted until finally there is no energy left in the management team. If investors own too large a proportion of a company, this is a reason in itself for not investing at all in a company, since those working there, the doers, will slowly but surely lose all motivation and finally leave.

It is important to invest sufficiently in the beginning, for several reasons. An unexpected but nevertheless common problem can arise in the first financing round if a relatively small amount of money is invested in the company. The entrepreneurs convert the capital into large values by working with tight margins, screwing suppliers, giving themselves low salaries, squeezing into small offices, and so on. But when the next investor enters to finance the continued expansion, which usually demands substantial sums of money, it happens that the investor in question thinks: a) the former investor injected too little money; or b) there is no substance (i.e. value) in the company considering the small initial investment. Frugality can cost and/or look bad. Not least when the next investor is international and used to seeing budgets from companies like Amazon.

Entrepreneurs who approach venture capitalists (both private individuals and companies), do not usually have much to show. Often just a business plan, maybe a demo or an overhead presentation. Investors can take advantage of this situation in order to come in at low cost – and with every right: this is when the risk, but also the return, is greatest. At the same time the company has to have enough money to get going. As founder, it is important to know what you need, and to stand up for it. The investors will probably say: 'This is just a PowerPoint presentation.' Then they will try to cut the price by half. Either you believe in the project and invest to the full or else you don't invest at all. Make sure you get enough money in from the start. What counts at the end of the day is the real money, money you can build companies with and pay bills with.

> **MAKE SURE YOU GET ENOUGH MONEY IN FROM THE START. WHAT COUNTS AT THE END OF THE DAY IS THE REAL MONEY, MONEY YOU CAN BUILD COMPANIES WITH AND PAY BILLS WITH**

It is just as much the entrepreneur choosing the right venture capitalist as it is the investors choosing which ideas to invest in. The investors will play a central role in the company's development for some time. An entrepreneur has to feel that they trust the investors and that they can contribute to the company's development.

A re-start, if it is a project within a large company or an established company undergoing a make-over, also lives on venture capital, in a manner of speaking. It depends on the stock market's and the owners' understanding that the money will be used for change and that the change is real. If financiers and owners don't understand, there will be no change.

The customers

Why do so many companies flop? They don't get any customers! Why don't they get any customers? Because the customers don't know why they should become customers! Why don't they understand why they should become customers? Because the offer is too complicated.

Now I would like to say something to all companies who invent smart, new business models, products and services:

There is a big difference between explaining a business model to venture capitalists and explaining it to customers.

Venture capitalists invest in the business model, but customers also have to invest in it in order for a start-up to get any revenues. Usually, customers do not understand where they should place their money, and so they move on. And this isn't the customers' problem, it is the company's. If you've built a business model, turn it upside down so that you can see if from the customer's perspective. That is the least you can do.

The same thing applies to a re-start. The old company that decides it needs to renew itself must not only convince its board and its owners, but also its customers.

The entrepreneur

The primary task for the entrepreneur and the company leader is to create value, both in terms of the valuation of the company (which the shareholders demand) and value to the customers. This is the trick: create value that can actually be transformed into real money, otherwise there is no economic foundation for the company. I accept that you have to experiment in order to find out what the company is good for, in the same way that we have experimented over the last couple of years with doing business on the net and tested different business models, but there is no durable economic development in businesses that can't convert value to revenues and, ultimately, profits. That's what working in a capitalist market is about. A company fails because the entrepreneur could not create value, revenue and profits.

The entrepreneur, the business leader, always has the ultimate responsibility. To believe anything else is naïve. Venture capitalists readily say that they are willing to help develop a start-up, which they do in many cases. Fondex would not have been able to start without the venture capital from IT Provider. But when it comes down to it, investors are nothing but investors, which is natural. Their role, like that of shareholders in a listed company, is to protect their investment (even though venture capitalists often participate actively in a company's development). An entrepreneur or company leader who doesn't understand that they have the ultimate responsibility for the company and who depends too much on others has not understood their role as implementor. Don't blame it on others.

Finally: You must be driven by your idea. Don't care too much about the money; the valuation of many companies is hypothetical anyway and often has nothing to do with real value. There is no such thing as easy money. Focus on making your idea successful, it will take all your time. If it works, money will follow automatically.

66 THERE IS NO SUCH THING AS EASY MONEY. FOCUS ON MAKING YOUR IDEA SUCCESSFUL, IT WILL TAKE ALL YOUR TIME. IF IT WORKS, MONEY WILL FOLLOW AUTOMATICALLY 99

The whole

A start-up or a re-start is like a Dutch treat. Everyone must bring something to the party. Someone brings the wine, someone else brings the dessert and a third brings the coffee. The host has an overall plan for the party, and the guests bring the parts. If everything works out, the result is a great party. If it doesn't work out, the party is a flop. What is it that makes the party a failure? People bring the wrong things, someone brings the right thing, but the wrong kind, someone doesn't bring enough (and the others look askance at the contribution: 'Look how little he brought with him …'), and someone forgets to bring their contribution but devours everyone else's. It can also be attributed to the host writing the wrong list, not having sufficient infrastructure for the project (i.e. not enough chairs and tables), or inviting the wrong people. At a Dutch treat, which is often a fairly small gathering, every guest is important. With common sense, generosity and good humor it often turns out to be a good party. But, as everyone knows, even parties that start off well can turn sour. It's all about finding the balance. The whole must work and everyone must be satisfied. And the music must be right – you need a groove to get the Movement going.

epilog

Fondex was sold in February 2000 to a British listed company. For Fondex, the purpose of the sale was a safer future for the company and funds for continued growth; it meant that the users and customers could look forward to receiving new, additional web services and it meant satisfied investors, who had invested time and money in the company. For the buyer, The Exchange Holdings, it meant access to a management team, technology, new services, and a platform for continued expansion.

Fondex had two major press conferences during its history. The first one was September 30 1998 when the company was still only a PowerPoint presentation and had just received financing. The second was February 28 2000, one and a half years later, when the deal with the new owner was made public. The deal was worth close to $50 million in shares and future funding.

The smaller company had become part of a larger company's continued growth, as it should be in a dynamic and perhaps chaotic economy. And perhaps more importantly, Fondex, which had been a start-up, run by entrepreneurs, had in a very short time become established and had entered a new phase.

In May 2000, the whole group changed its name to Moneyextra plc, the consumer brand of The Exchange, and the plan was to build a pan-European portal for personal finance. The plans came to nothing when the dot com market collapsed, and in November 2000, the group announced the sale of the consumer business, including Fondex, and a name change back to Exchange FS (for financial systems). In winter 2001, the Swedish financial online market was consolidating. Fondex was acquired by internet broker TeleTrade, which then merged with another broker, Nordnet, to form one of Scandinavia's largest trading services on the web. The changes never stop in a dynamic market.

bibliography

Branson, R., **Losing My Virginity – The Autobiography,** London: Virgin Publishing Ltd,1998.

Bronson, P., **The Nudist on the Late Shift – And Other True Tales of Silicon Valley,** New York: Random House, 1999.

Deal, T. and Kennedy, A., **Corporate Cultures – The Rites and Rituals of Corporate Life,** Reading, Mass: Addison-Wesley Publishing Company, 1982.

Grove, A., **Only the Paranoid Survive,** New York: Doubleday, 1996.

Kelly, K., 'The economics of ideas.' **Wired,** June 1996.

Kelly, K., **New Rules for the New Economy: 10 Radical Strategies for a Connected World,** 1999.

McLuhan, M. and Fiore, Q., **The Medium is the Message – An Inventory of Effects,** New York: Bantam Books, 1967.

Moore, G., **Crossing the Chasm – Marketing and Selling High-Tech Products to Mainstream Customers,** New York: Harper Business, 1991.

Nielsen, J., **Designing Web Usability – The Practice of Simplicity,** Indianapolis: New Riders Publishing, 1999.

Normann, R., **Service Management – Strategy and Leadership in Service Business,** 2nd ed, Chichester: Wiley, 1991.

Roberts, P., 'Getting it done.' **Fast Company,** June 2000.

Schwartz, P., **The Art of the Long View – Planning for the Future in an Uncertain World,** New York: Doubleday, 1991.

Shakespeare, W., **Hamlet,** 1601.

Sloan, A. P., Jr, **My Years with General Motors,** 1996.

index

Thank you

Jennifer, my wife, for your support

My parents, Barbro and Carl-Johan,
without whom I would be nothing

Bertil Ekerlid, my Swedish publisher

Richard Stagg, my English publisher at FT.com/Pearson Education,
Penelope Allport, my project manager, and all those who played a part
in the editorial production of this book

To the best teams I have worked with:

Fondex
Simon Lindfors, Teddy Belin, Jesper Strandberg, Ola Kellander, Per Carlsson,
Malin Björkmo, and the rest of the company

IT Provider
Lars Johansson, Johan Hernmarck, Per Wejke, Håkan Ramsin

Icon Medialab
Johan Staël von Holstein, Jesper Jos Olsson, Erik Wickström

SMG
Richard Normann, Bo Ekman, Dag Norén, Anders Holst,
Björn Westerberg, Henrik Ankarcrona

Moneyextra
Carlo Barravalle, Paul Lindsey, Nigel Phillips